The Pleasure of
Antiques

The Pleasure of
Antiques

Gold and Silver,
Glass and Furniture,
Pottery and Porcelain,
Clocks and Watches

J.C. Wardell-Yerburgh

OCTOPUS BOOKS

For Atlanta

First published 1974 by
Octopus Books Limited
59 Grosvenor Street, London W1

ISBN 0 7064 0327 4

© 1974 Octopus Books Limited

Produced by
Mandarin Publishers Limited
14 Westlands Road,
Quarry Bay, Hong Kong
Printed in Hong Kong

Contents

1
Antiquities & Early Antiques

People are interested in antiques for a number of reasons. One person will buy a single item for its beauty, regardless of its rarity, whilst another will buy an article specifically to make a profit reselling it. Many collectors specialize in one particular field; even more confine themselves to one period or one country. Whatever one's interest, some knowledge of the parallel developments of various branches of design and craftsmanship will expand and enrich that interest.

This book is concerned with five different types of antiques up to the year 1830—pottery and porcelain; gold and silver; glass; furniture; clocks and watches. It is within these broad categories that the finest craftsmanship in the decorative arts has been shown.

The first section also takes in some of the antiquities of the ancient civilizations, the European Middle Ages and the Eastern cultures. While not falling within the usually accepted range of 'antiques', they belong here because of their profound influence on the designs and styles of succeeding generations throughout the world. And antiquities are not without interest to the potential collector; some are still collectable since they are still being found.

Although there is very little Egyptian furniture extant—only what has been preserved in a few tombs— we know what it was like from scenes depicted in tomb murals and paintings. This panel of wood overlaid with gold foil shows Tutankhamun seated on a wooden folding stool attended by his wife. His feet rest on a footstool, while she has to make do with a cushion. The legs of some folding stools terminated in ducks' heads, others in lions' paws like this one. The cushioned seats were usually of leather. Egyptian furniture we know of included beds, stools, chairs and chests.

PREVIOUS PAGES *Rooms even in great houses were still only sparsely furnished as late as the 16th century. Most of the rich effect here, in the Palazzo Davanzati in Florence, comes from the boldly carved ceiling and the colourful wall paintings, whose* trompe l'oeil *technique is so skilled that one could easily believe them to be real wall hangings. To the modern taste the room looks very uncomfortable, but there would have been cushions, carpets and rugs. It contains a simple Renaissance-type table, with four matching chairs. The rest of the furniture, all of polished wood, comprises two large storage chests, two hard chairs, a pair of bellows by the fireplace, and an early type of sofa, evolved from the* cassone *(marriage chest).*

Antiques are defined today as objects over one hundred years old, which is a relatively new classification. The year 1830 has been chosen as cutoff point because during the last three-quarters of the nineteenth century, makers of fine things largely followed a series of revivals of styles from earlier periods. For this reason it can be considered a less significant period in the history of antiques. It is, however, an extremely significant period in the history of antique-collecting, because it was precisely during this newly machine-dominated age, as copies proliferated, that originals became widely sought after and appreciated.

Although great collections had been started among the very rich as early as the sixteenth century, it was not until the 'Grand Tour' drew the attention of travellers to the arts of other countries, that the less wealthy were prepared for the first time to pay more for the old than for the new. And as many of the richest families followed the twists and turns of fashion, replacing one style with another, their 'discards' became available for acquisition by those below them on the economic scale. In this way, the circle of people interested in antiques, for their diverse reasons, has become an ever-widening one.

By the same token, as original works became more valuable, copies were made more accurately and were passed off as originals. Faking became good business and was a major hazard to the collector. Every collector must always be on guard against fakes. They are obviously more common in more expensive pieces and here special care—and expert advice—should be taken. In furniture pieces are often 'made up', and it is important to know about the methods of old joiners and the sort of screws they used, and to be able to recognize genuine handles, hinges etc. Similar hazards await collectors of silver, porcelain, glass, and other objects. The only general advice can be: always examine an object with great care, and if there is something that seems out of place or out of character, beware; always take expert advice if you are making an expensive purchase.

Simple pottery objects are characteristic of a very early stage of human civilization, but techniques of shaping, painting and glazing can make it a very sophisticated art. Pottery, or earthenware, is made from clay, which varies in colour from white to reddish-brown, and in texture from coarse to very fine. The technique of throwing clay on a wheel was also known to many ancient peoples. The potter uses his hands to achieve the required shape as the wheel spins, or in the case of a tiny vessel, he can use a small tool. A lathe is then sometimes used for refinements.

Solid objects were made in clay moulds. Figures were made in sections and fused together with wet clay. Techniques of glazing were later discovered to seal the porous surface and enhance the beauty of pottery. Glazes may be of many colours, either opaque or translucent.

Perhaps the finest early pottery which can still be collected was made in Greece in the millennium before Christ. The earliest vessels had mainly geometric decoration, but around the sixth century BC potters began to paint designs of figures using the 'black-figure' technique and later the 'red-figure' technique. It is to the ornamental motifs and figured scenes of the Corinthian and Athenian potters that we are indebted for much information about contemporary dress, furniture and social life.

Porcelain was first produced by the Chinese around AD 700, and they guarded the secret so well that they kept their monopoly until the early seventeenth century. When perfect, porcelain is hard, resonant to the strike, white and translucent when held against a strong light. It is achieved by mixing kaolin, a white china clay, with petuntze, a china stone of the generic group of rocks called felspar. A felspathic glaze used on hard-paste porcelain is made from the same material.

The early Chinese porcelain contained petuntze from different rock beds, which had an assortment of impurities, difficult to remove with primitive refinement techniques. This meant that the porcelain varied with the effect of the impurities it contained. Thus, unless the actual rock bed is known, it is difficult to imitate early specimens. When the mixture of kaolin and petuntze is fired at the correct temperature (1450°C, 2650°F) in a kiln, true hard-paste porcelain results.

So-called soft-paste porcelain, which was first introduced into Europe at the end of the sixteenth century (hard-paste porcelain was finally discovered in the early eighteenth century), is not in fact a true porcelain, although it enabled European factories to imitate Chinese wares more successfully than with plain earthenware. For both earthenware and soft pastes non-felspathic glazes are used, which are in fact a kind of glass. Paints applied to certain ceramics before they are glazed are called underglaze colours. If they are applied after the glaze, usually because they cannot stand the full heat of the kiln, they are called overglaze or enamel colours.

Gold and silver have always been symbolic of wealth, and sought after for the lustre they hold, their durability and their malleability. In fact they are too soft by themselves to attain proper toughness and they must therefore be alloyed to small proportions of other heavy metals, such as copper or platinum.

Gold is either mined or washed with water from auriferous gold-yielding deposits, or sluiced. A sluice is a long sloping channel with constant running water, having a series of transverse bars to trap the gold, whose high density will cause it to sink. The Romans found that lining the trenches in the sluice with mercury resulted in a gold amalgam from which the mercury could subsequently be removed by heat. The cleaned gold ore must be powdered before the metal can be extracted, again by washing.

The colour of gold varies according to the quantity and type of alloy. Copper makes it redder, silver makes it greenish, and the addition of both copper and silver will produce a yellower tone than that of pure gold. White gold is three parts of gold mixed with one of platinum. The purity of gold today is measured in its carat value, that is the number of parts of pure gold in twenty-four; thus eighteen carat gold means eighteen parts of gold to six parts alloy, and the higher the carat the purer the gold.

Most silver is extracted from lead ore. The silver is purified from the ore by fractional melting, as lead has a much lower melting point. To purify gold and silver, temperatures of 1065°C, 1950°F and 1000°C, 1830°F respectively are needed. Wood fires can only achieve heats of around 700°C, 1290°F, which reddens but does not melt the metals. Therefore true metal working did not begin until higher temperatures became attainable with the use of artificial stimulation of the fire in the form of the furnace.

The discovery of glass-making is in the realm of legend. According to Pliny the secret was first discovered by chance when some sailors, who had made a fire on a sandy beach, noticed that by fusing sand (silica) with soda (alkali) and lime (calcium carbonate) a vitreous (glasslike) glaze resulted. They also found that if it was made thick enough it would not collapse, and it could be cut into small pieces for decoration, called mosaics. The paste could be pressed into open earthenware or metal moulds to make solid objects. Hollow vessels were made around sand cores, which were later removed. The oldest surviving glass objects are gaily coloured beads made of pebbles coated with glass. These were exported all over the Mediterranean world from Egypt, Syria and Phoenicia from the fourth century BC.

The secret of glass blowing was discovered about 100 BC, probably also by chance, and this would have happened when a solid rod, used to hold the molten blob of glass, was replaced by a hollow tube. After that the amount of glass required was picked up red hot and quickly blown up to the right size. The vessel was shaped with accessory instruments, and handles and spouts sometimes added. From this period many objects survive, principally the ointment jars and larger vessels recovered undamaged from burial chambers, together with pottery objects.

During the first four centuries AD two separate traditions emerged. The Syrians, who are credited with the discovery of glass blowing, made simple objects like flasks and scent bottles, first in shades of green and yellow, and later in blues and purples. Decoration was naturalistic, and vases appear in the guise of shells or fruits, or moulded with human masks. Roman glassmakers, who also settled and worked in Alexandria, were more advanced, especially in their ability to control bright colours. They knew how to draw with an engraving tool and developed the arts of cutting the surface with grooves and facets from inside and out, and of carving in relief. A speciality was to carve and undercut at the same time so that the finished object looked as though it had a lacy coating attached by a series of tiny bridges. Sometimes pieces were carved, cut and coloured. Another technique was that of laying opaque glass on a coloured base. It was then cut and ground away, leaving a cameo design in white against a deep coloured background. The finest example is the Portland vase, a black two-handled vessel decorated with white cameos.

Furnaces were simple to set up, and wherever the Roman armies conquered, glassmaking spread, so that glass from the Roman period can be found throughout most of Europe and North Africa.

The earliest known furniture is that recovered from Egyptian tombs, followed by objects depicted on Greek pottery. The ancient Greeks were not wide-ranging in their forms. They concentrated on a few simple but elegant shapes, while perfecting the crafts of gilding, carving, and joinery. Furniture was made from both native and imported timbers: maple, beech, cedar, oak and sycamore were among those available to them. Many of the thrones, couches and chests made by

Here is a rare example of a Byzantine drinking vessel, said to have been in the possession of Lorenzo de' Medici. It was probably acquired by an Italian during the sack of Constantinople. The bowl is of mottled sardonyx in varying shades of brown and white, hollowed out and ribbed on the outside. The gold lining is folded over to form an outer lip, which is tooled with two rows of beading, enclosing a band of stars and trimmed with pierced petal shapes. The ribbing is repeated on the gold knop, which broadens out into a trumpet stem.

the Greeks show Egyptian influence. These items, together with chairs, tables and footstools appear to be all they considered necessary.

Typical features that recur on Egyptian, Greek and Roman furniture are animal forms for table supports and chair legs and backs, in particular swans, lions and winged sphinxes. Greek chairs, with their elegant sabre legs, have been prototypes for many succeeding generations, as have couches and marble-topped tables found at Herculaneum and Pompeii.

The first clocks were sundials and obelisks, both dependent on the presence of daylight and sunshine. An obelisk is a tall stone needle which throws a shadow on a marked area when the sun shines. Other means of measuring time were water clocks, candles burning, and sand pouring, generally against a calibrated scale.

With the disintegration of the Roman Empire around AD 500 classical culture as such was destroyed by the barbarian invaders, though many elements were preserved in the Byzantine Empire, founded in the fourth century, which grew and prospered throughout the medieval period. From the beginning its art was dedicated to the principle that the Emporor was God's representative on earth. Consequently the flavour of its culture is strongly religious. Lives of saints and biblical scenes are depicted on silver dishes, glass vessels, ivory carvings, mosaics, manuscripts, silk tapestries and metalwork of all kinds from many parts of the Byzantine Empire. Some lovely pieces of jewel-coloured glassware, now in St Mark's, Venice, were looted from Constantinople in the Fourth Crusade in 1204.

The major Islamic art forms with which we are concerned are pottery and glass. The Arabs, who by the eighth century ruled lands stretching from Spain to India, had very little culture of their own and were quick to absorb those of Egypt, Greece, Rome, Persia and Mesopotamia. In glass, the tradition of Alexandria was continued; thick, dark-coloured glass resembling precious stones was made and engraved with figurative decorations. The important centres were Rakka on the Euphrates, and Samarra and Baghdad on the Tigris. Decorations were similar to those on contemporary Persian and Egyptian ceramics. Violet coloured Aleppo glass came from Syria and was enhanced with floral patterns and geometrical designs, and glass made in Damascus was distinctly Chinese in feeling. It was in Damascus and Baghdad that the techniques of enamelling were brought to perfection. The finest mosque lamps were made in Persia and Syria, vase-shaped hanging vessels decorated with Arabic heraldry and inscriptions, from which they can often be dated.

The early Islamic pottery, while not so technically perfect as the cold, hard enamels of contemporary Chinese porcelain, was warmer in feeling and more subdued. Shapes were simple, decoration harmonious. Floral and geometric motifs, spread over the whole surface, were the common form of decoration, since Islamic religion forbade the representation of living creatures.

The Chinese particularly excelled in all forms of ceramic art. Pottery of the T'ang period is renowned for its beautiful shapes and controlled use of strong colours. The T'ang potters' lead-glazed figures of animals and people are highly prized today because of their simple lines and fine proportions. The period of the Sung dynasty (AD 960-1279) produced many new developments, notably the soft green celadon stoneware, and the Kuan type with its fine crackled glaze.

Side by side with the pottery industry, porcelain was produced, and during the Ming dynasty (AD 1368-1644) both branches flourished, much being exported. The designs of flowers, birds, and figured scenes were first produced in three colours and then five, together with the fabled blue and white. Towards the end of the Ming period the 'famille' rose, noire, verte and jaune began to appear. These families were groups of porcelains having one dominant colour in the general scheme, and were described ecstatically by returning travellers.

The decorative arts of the European Middle Ages reflected the dominant styles of architecture. There were considerable commercial developments, and during the period 1100 to 1400, the first guilds of craftsmen were formed for protection against illegal and inferior competitors. Trading towns sprang up, and trade between nations increased in the way to which the East had long been accustomed. Leagues of trading cities were established, and with the rise of a merchant middle class, luxury goods were made for a larger public.

The earliest furniture of the Middle Ages was often plain and crude, though attempts to disguise the fact were made by painting it, and colourful hangings and carpets from the Middle East and fine textiles from Italy were draped on walls and tables to soften the effect. The main item to be found in every large house was the marriage chest. French ones were sometimes covered with iron scrollwork; the English decorated theirs with arched panelling and Gothic motifs derived from church architecture, as did the Dutch and Germans. Italian cassoni carved and painted were the finest of all.

In northern Europe, most furniture was made from oak, but chestnut, walnut and cypress were more plentiful in Italy, southern France and Spain. Pine furniture naturally predominated in Alpine regions.

Very little fine pottery was produced in Europe in the Middle Ages outside Spain. The Arabs imposed Islamic traditions and introduced the arts of tin-glazed (a white pottery glaze) and lustred earthenware. The latter were vases and dishes glazed with the metallic lustre of copper or silver. These wares are usually known as Hispano-Moresque. A speciality was to paint the arms of a family in a circle of foliage or petals. After this idea caught on among Italian noblemen Italian craftsmen began to make their own imitations, and they were followed by other Europeans.

The gradual decline of Islamic glass coincided with the establish-

It is thought that this elaborate gold and jasper salt was made for Louis XI of France about 1460. Typically Gothic in style, its eight arches support the upper base, decorated with filigree work. Two enamelled figurines grace the stem and the bowl is of jasper. Salts were social segregators on medieval long tables, when the lord and lady shared their meals with the retainers. Dependants and other inferiors sat below the salt, persons of rank above it.

ment of the Venetian glassworks in 1291 on the island of Murano. During the fourteenth century the glass industry of Murano continued to produce coloured wares, and started to make glass mirrors, replacing those of polished metal. Rather poor quality bubble-ridden glassware for the table was also made, but it was not until the sixteenth century that something approaching clear crystal glass was achieved.

By 1400 the techniques of working precious metals were well advanced. As with furniture, the style in Germany, northern Europe and England reflected contemporary Gothic architecture. Decoration frequently included precious stones, Gothic lettering and entire enamelled figurines of saints. Tracery is reminiscent of that on thrones and pulpits, while designs of foot supports and finials of vessels were copied from the crockets and pinnacles of contemporary stonework.

Fine quality tooling occurred on flat metalwork (plate) provided it was thin enough. Five terms are often used loosely, and need clarification: *punching* refers to indentations on the surface made by a plain or shaped punch. *Embossing* means decoration raised up in relief on the upper surface from the back. *Chasing* is in effect embossing from the front. When elaborate scenes and patterns contained both embossed and chased relief, this is referred to as *repoussé*. The process called *gilding* is the application of gold on to the surface of baser metals including silver. It was known in ancient times, and by the Middle Ages was in such common use that it encouraged fraudulent practices: any metal could be passed off as gold. Gold and silver alloys could also contain more base metals than necessary without it being apparent. Thus the first guilds were largely occupied with devising tests and enforcing regulations whereby a standard could be guaranteed. The only controls stringent enough were those by the English.

A French cabinet of solid walnut, carved and gilded, c. 1550. It is inlaid with marble panels and stands on bun feet. The distinctly architectural construction, making use of elongated Doric columns, is characteristic of Renaissance furniture, and the carvings of bizarre masks set in formalized foliage offer a perfect example of the 'grotesque' decoration which was derived from the arts of Antiquity.

The first flowering of the Renaissance was in the Italian city states, which were well provided with wealthy banking families inclined to patronize the arts. The rediscovery of ancient civilizations led to a new affinity with Classical antiquity. A style based on the purer forms of Greece and Rome emerged, and Italian craftsmen were lured to the important European centres to diffuse their ideas and their skills.

Furniture, even in the great palaces, was still sparse, and depended on lavish use of upholstery and hangings for colour and richness. Cupboards and chests were made to look like monuments with columnar supports. *Cassoni* took on a sarcophagus-like appearance of Egyptian derivation. With the addition of wings and backs to simple seats, the first sofas were created. Greater use of figurative carving was made and the first bronze handles appeared on cupboards. Painted scenes were still a form of decoration; gradually the triumphs of Roman generals gained favour over religious scenes as subject

matter. Wood was both polished and gilded (gold on wood) and magnificent marble-topped tables mounted on richly carved supports were made for the great houses. Decorative motifs included sphinxes, nymphs and masks amid elaborate arrangements of foliage, together with human and mythological figures. As the style gradually spread northwards, each country developed its own interpretations.

Renaissance silver and silver gilt lost the Gothic formality of the preceding centuries, and new, intricate designs of strapwork and *repoussé* were used. The ideas of the great Italian silversmith Benvenuto Cellini (1500-69) spread to France and then England; and to the few pieces of domestic plate (salts, ewers and basins, and tall drinking cups) were added beakers and tankards, spoons, and flatware. Two-handled cups appeared, the handles often in the form of elongated human torsos, with decorations including mythological scenes and other motifs derived from Roman murals.

Venetian Murano continued to dominate the European glass industry. There, in addition to *cristallo*, or crystal glass, a milky white glass known as *lattimo* was developed, which was a good base for enamelling. Perhaps Murano's most notable success was filigree glass, sometimes called *reticello* or *vetro di trina*, with what appeared to be a network of opaque threads, white at first and later coloured. The quality of crystal glass improved; it became less cloudy and bubbly. In glass tableware Venice enjoyed a virtual monopoly for some time.

The style of the Renaissance is reflected in contemporary tin-glazed pottery produced both in Spain (particularly in the area around Valencia) and in the new Italian centres of Umbria, Tuscany and Emilia. Faenza, the most important of the towns, gave its name to the product (*faenza* or *faience*). Decorations were in bright colours depicting mythological and biblical subjects, contained in borders of strapwork and other Renaissance motifs. The industry spread to Antwerp, Holland and finally England, and was variously called 'maiolica' and 'delft' in addition to 'faience'.

Increasing trade led to a need for better timekeeping. The first mechanical clocks appeared on buildings in public places at the end of the thirteenth century, and are known as monumental clocks. Mechanical clocks were made possible by the invention of the verge escapement, which allows the driving power to escape systematically by a series of teeth. The source of energy was provided by a weight. Mechanical clocks were developed rapidly, both technically and artistically, particularly in Augsburg and Nuremberg; thereafter in Switzerland, France, Italy and England. From these public clocks were evolved the early household clocks, at first made by blacksmiths in cast iron. Cases were decorated in the Gothic style with pinnacles, scrolls, crockets, and ornamental pediments, and later with mythological and allegorical scenes in keeping with the Renaissance.

The next stage in clock development began with the invention of the spring-driven motor which replaced weights. Its advantages were that clocks could store power for longer periods, and were more easily portable. However, the problem with springs is that they do not unwind evenly, that is, power is released faster to begin with, and slower towards the end. Therefore a means of regulating them had to be devised. The *fusée*, which was invented in France in 1530 and incorporated into watches ten years later, solved the problem to some extent; it consisted of a conical-shaped grooved drum round which a length of gut was so arranged as to ensure the even unwinding of the main spring.

Cases were made of chased and gilded silver and copper, and clockmakers indulged their fantasies in devising a variety of decoration, including people and animals. By the fifteenth century hourly and quarterly chimes, alarms, and an assortment of astronomical elaborations had been added to the basic timepiece. The needs of travellers were met by cylindrical clocks in hard leather cases, adapted to cope with the jolting movement of a horse-drawn carriage. Later they were made like watches as we know them but larger, thicker and drum-shaped. By about 1510 the movements were made small enough to be carried in the pocket, or on a chain round the neck. Early iron movements were replaced by brass, because the latter was rust-free.

Above A typical Phoenician glass jug, made in about 500 BC. Pliny's story of the discovery of glass was told of Phoenician sailors, and, whether or not this is true, Phoenician river mouths were rich in seaweed and coastal plants, from which the necessary soda could be taken. Quantities of glass beads, amphoras, ointment jars and vases have been found in the Mediterranean countries, all made in a technically similar manner, and usually decorated with some variety of linear pattern, wavy lines, zig-zags, concentric circles or palmettes.

Left Although the principal pottery centres in mainland Greece were near Athens and Corinth, there were countless provincial centres and the fact that Greek pots have been found as far afield even as southern Russia testifies also to the flourishing export trade. This hydria was found in Caere (Cerveteri) in Etruria and it is thought to be one of a group painted by an Ionian Greek in about 530 BC. The scenes are painted in the black-figure technique: the figures were painted in black slip (clay particles suspended in water), and the details were incised into the clay after this had dried; it was then fired to a glossy black finish. In the later red-figure technique the background was painted in black, leaving the figures as silhouettes in the reddish-brown clay; the details were then added with much greater subtlety by the artist's brush. Depicted here are Odysseus and his companion blinding the cyclops Polyphemos.

Right Greenish tinted Roman glass vases have survived in considerable quantity and are among the antiquities most readily available to the collector. They were blown rather than made round a sand core, this one, made *c.*AD 100, having a broad flange (lip) at the opening, and below the long neck a globular body flattened at the bottom. The iridescence on the glass is caused by the action of ammonia salts in the air or in the earth, which, in the presence of moisture, decompose the glass, forming soluble carbonate of soda or potash. As this is worn from the surface, tiny flakes remain, which break up light rays to give the irridescent effect.

Top A drinking vessel made in Mexico from half a gourd, lacquered with red inside and black outside. Lacquering was a native Mexican craft, the lacquer being made from chia seed oil and red earth, which produced a durable glossy waterproof finish. The gourd is set in a simple silver mount of the Spanish Colonial period, *c.*1550, but may itself be pre-Spanish, since the dimly visible design was a pattern common in pre-Columbian times, but generally replaced after the conquest by designs from Spain.

Above This is an example of what an advanced but pre-industrial society has made. The Hausa tribe have lived for centuries, and still live, along the south edge of the Sahara Desert, notably in northern Nigeria, Niger, and Dahomey. Their homes are semi-permanent mud constructions, easily repaired, which they decorate with paint or low relief moulding. In this example the roof is constructed of interwoven palm fronds. These interior walls are bare; some of them have been found to be decorated with mud sculpture, paints, and occasionally blue and white porcelains from China (traded for ivory and gold). The bed is also constructed of mud and built into the wall of the hut.

Left Stirrup pots, so called because of the shape of the spouts, are characteristic of the pottery found in Ecuador, Peru and Columbia, and rarely in North America. They have little practical use, and were ceremonial or funerary vessels, sometimes filled with wine; some of them emit a low whistling sound when liquid is poured from them. These are of the Mochican people, who lived along the west coast of Peru, and date from around AD 600. The vessels represent a warrior carrying a shield and a weapon, a woman holding a child, and a turbaned man playing a flute.

Above left Vase-shaped hanging mosque lamps were made throughout Islamic lands in glass and pottery. These colours are typical of the Turkish pottery made at Iznik (Nicaea). They frequently carry an inscription from the Koran; this one reads 'God is the Light of Heaven and Earth resembling a lamp shining in a recess in the wall'. The lamp comes from the Suleimaniyeh mosque at Constantinople, which was completed in 1556. Mosque lamps were also made in glass, the best known being Syrian, and also bore inscriptions from the Koran, with decorations in blue, green, red and gold.

Above right Bowls of Sari ware were produced in Persia in the late 10th and early 11th centuries. This one, which has straight flaring sides, is decorated in manganese purple, brown, yellow and green, in an easy, restful style typical of Islamic potters. Observe how the bird is the central feature in the design, yet we are not forced to notice it; it merges with the whole picture. Islamic craftsmen were more interested in line, play of light, and design than were their Chinese contemporaries, whose preoccupation was with perfection of form and quality of paste; Islamic ceramics are more brittle than the Chinese and have a coarser feel.

Below left Only three examples of Ming wine jars such as this one are known. Dating from the 14th century, it belongs to a much admired group of porcelains made at the factories of Ch'ing-tê-chên under the Mongol invaders. It is 13¼ inches high. It combines the techniques of painting in underglaze cobalt blue with the new idea of imitating on porcelain the openwork panels of medieval Near Eastern metalwork. Flowers of the four seasons, pre-moulded, are adhered with clay on to low stilts and glazed in copper red within quatrefoil panels.

Right The T'ang dynasty bridges the years AD 618-906, which for China was a period of peace and prosperity. The ceramics of this period were usually covered with a thick shiny coloured glaze, though some pieces made of a coarse whitish material were left unglazed and painted with gay pigments. Many terracotta statuettes survive, most of them removed from tombs. Most sought after are animals, such as horses and camels, and humans, like the lady shown here with her round face surmounted by an elaborate headdress in the form of a bird. Be on your guard with T'ang pieces as many copies have been made from the 19th century to the present day.

Opposite Italian *cassoni*, used to store the family linens and clothes, were frequently made in pairs to commemorate a marriage; a few were accompanied by a *spallaera*, the part which hangs on the wall above. This is the bride's half of the pair made for the marriage in 1472 of Lorenzo di Matteo de Morelli and Vagia di Tania de Francesco de' Nerli in Florence; the arms of both families are painted on the side panels. The finest artists of Renaissance Italy devoted their talents to the decoration of such *cassoni*, often with religious subjects, though events from the early history of Rome are depicted here.

Above right French coffers made in the second half of the 13th century were often decorated with wrought iron scrollwork, which served to strengthen the construction and camouflage to some extent the simple joinery of heavy oak planks. Iron volutes like those on chests are also found on cathedral doors of the same period. Not all French chests were decorated in this way, many are carved with elaborate Gothic arcading and scenes of chivalry, with knights in armour jousting or in battle.

Right Chairs of X-shape construction appear early in the history of European furniture; they were popular all over the Continent in the 14th and 15th centuries, as we know from manuscripts and paintings, although few survive. Originally designed to fold, they evolved into the type shown here with a fixed back. This one is said to have belonged to Girolamo Savonarola (1452-98), the Italian preacher and reformer, whose uncompromising ideals and passionate oratory led to his imprisonment for heresy and finally to the gallows.

Left Under all the rigging, these silver ships, known as nefs, were usually wine vessels. They were made in the Middle Ages and the finest examples come from Germany and Switzerland. One is recorded in a papal inventory of 1392. Every detail of the ship is faithfully reproduced; in the fighting tops little figures stand guard, while other sailors are busy on deck, or clambering up rope ladders. When the whole thing was tilted, the wine poured out of the figurehead, in this case a dragon. Later nefs were also used to accommodate the napkin, knife and spoon of their owners.

Above right The basic shape of an animal horn lends itself to drinking vessels. The Saxons used both complete horns and beakers which were made from a section of the horn with a bottom inserted. In the later Middle Ages drinking horns were largely discarded, but along with coconuts and other curious or barbaric objects they were quite frequently mounted in precious metals and used as guild presentation pieces (*see also* the Mexican gourd on p. 15). This horn is German, made around 1450 and exquisitely mounted in silver-gilt.

Below left The Gothic style is evident in this German silver-gilt chalice, a piece of church plate made *c.*1380. The small funnel-shaped cup is mounted above a knop studded with six enamelled lozenges below chased leaves. Above and below are two inscriptions: 'Got Liep' and 'Maria Liep'. The trumpet stem has a stepped foot and embossed figures of worshippers adoring the Virgin and Child, under a scroll inscribed 'Maria bis mir genadig' (Mary be gracious to me). Round the foot the lettering reads 'Margaret Lorge Sperling von Leyden'. The Gothic style in German ecclesiastical plate survived until around 1600.

Below right The Gloucester candlestick, as this fine piece is called, is thought to have been made in England *c.*1110 and later to have passed into the possession of Le Mans Cathedral in France. The inscription tells us it was given to the Abbey (now the Cathedral of St Peter), Gloucester, by Peter, who was Abbot from 1104 to 1131. The openwork of interlaced foliage and human or grotesque animal figures in gilt bell metal is typical of the work of 12th-century goldsmiths.

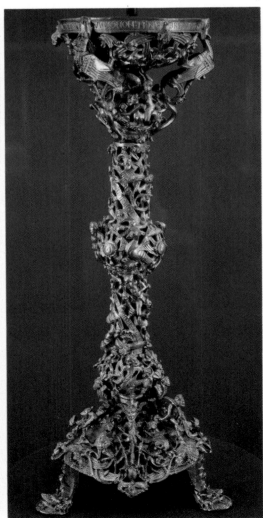

Left The Murano goblet shown here was made about 1480, and shows the influence of the Renaissance, to which glass-makers also contributed. The deep blue glass is one of a range of bright jewel-like colours first developed in Alexandria and Islamic territories, others being emerald green, amethyst and red. The decoration was usually religious (as here), mythological or allegorical. Additional motifs were medallions, floral crowns and, occasionally, representations of great men.

Right The maiolica industry in Tuscany was established in the 13th century. This fine jug was probably made in the Urbino area between 1550 and 1600. The handle takes the form of a serpent and the entire surface of the vessel is decorated with cherubs set against a white tin glaze in the style known as 'Bianchi di Faenza' and with grotesques typical of those produced at the Cafaggiolo factory near Florence. This factory, established in 1506, had formerly been the home of a junior branch of the Medici family.

Below This kind of tin-glazed earthenware bottle, or *aquamanile*, about 9 inches high and 11 inches long, is typical of those produced in the area around Valencia in Spain *c.*1510. The light buff-coloured earthenware is decorated in a copper lustre with a repeated Latin inscription and geometric patterns, while the front bears a heraldic emblem in a pattern of flowers and leaves such as was popular with the great French and Italian families. Other types of early Valencia ware were decorated by Moorish potters in blue and white designs and gold lustre.

Above left This group of furniture was recovered from a hunting lodge of King James I, which has been demolished. The table is oak, carved and inlaid with sycamore, bog oak and other woods, and was made in England *c.*1600. The massive bulbous legs were copied from German and Flemish pattern books. The table has a draw leaf, which extends it to twice the closed length. On one side is an oak carved bench, with turned legs, and on the other are a pair of stools, similarly made.

Below left Elizabethan architectural beds like this magnificent four-poster are typical of English Renaissance furniture. They were usually made of oak, though here the material used is walnut. The wood is inlaid with holly and bog oak on the headboard and on the elaborately carved frieze, which bears the date 1593 together with the initials RC. The frieze of the tester is inlaid with crows, the crest of the Corbet family. The bed would originally have had colourful hangings, probably imported from Italy.

Right Elaborately carved furniture originated in Italy, and by the second half of the 16th century had spread to France and Spain. This fall-front *escritoire*, carved from solid walnut, was made in the reign of Charles V (1516-56), Spain's golden age. The front drops onto slides, which pull out, terminating in *putti* on horses. The walnut is inlaid with contrasting panels of burr walnut, enclosed in architectural frames; the centre ones are cross-banded with orangewood. The angles are carved with pairs of figures and masks, and the top half is divided into small drawers and doors, each of which is decorated with an inset figure.

Left Early cast-iron chamber clocks equipped with 'Jacks' for striking the bell were extremely rare. This example, made *c*.1580, is decorated with the heraldry of its owner. The figure surmounting the clock, the 'Jack', strikes the hours on the large bell with the hammer he holds in his hands, and at the quarter hours, he kicks the two smaller bells with his heels. This is achieved by a system of levers set in motion by the striking mechanism. Clocks like these would have stood on a bracket attached to the wall and were driven by weights.

Right The Strasbourg clock, made by Isaac Habrecht in 1589, is in the form of a three-storey tower of gilded copper, with numerous allegorical figures peopling the top storey. The large plate at the bottom moves round its whole circuit only once a year; the outer ring shows the date of the month and all the church feasts and holy days in the year; the smaller ring represents the twelve signs of the Zodiac with the sun and moon, and the central circle represents a globe. The small dial on the second storey shows the minutes and the minute hand. On each side are two silver figures, and when the clock strikes, one figure turns the hour glass and the other wields the sickle of death. The hour hand completes a twenty-four hour circuit on the upper dial, each half of the dial plate containing twelve hours. On the third storey the various temporal allegories include a representation of the Day of Judgment. At the top of the filigree copper dome is a cock which spreads its wings and crows as the clock strikes.

Below Early watches were sometimes set in cases of hardstones, such as crystal, agate or amethyst. This example, housed in a case of hollowed emerald, was made *c*.1595 and is reputed to have been in the possession of the French royal family. It has a verge movement and there are half-hour divisions on the dial, which is unusual as there were generally quarter-hour divisions. The inner case is of brass-gilt, and the cover is pierced to reveal the numerals. The dial is of pierced silver, the single hand of blued steel, and the movement is of brass. The watch would drop out of the casing to be wound from the back.

2

The
BaroqueAge

In the seventeenth century the decorative arts followed the trends of contemporary architecture, and the style that emerged from the more complex forms of the Renaissance was essentially elaborate, highly decorated and ponderous: the Baroque. Still drawing on Classical antiquity for its ideas, it represented at the same time a revolt against the freshness and purity of classicism. Sweeping curves and resplendent ornament became the order of the day, and while the style may be thought vulgar and theatrical, it was yet symmetrical and exuberant.

The Baroque must be viewed against the social background of Italy, where it developed. Here, as in the rest of Europe, there now existed a bourgeoisie, comprising bankers, traders and merchants, eager to buy their way into the circle of great families. In the rivalry between the old and the new aristocracies, ostentation and the desire to impress took precedence over comfort and taste.

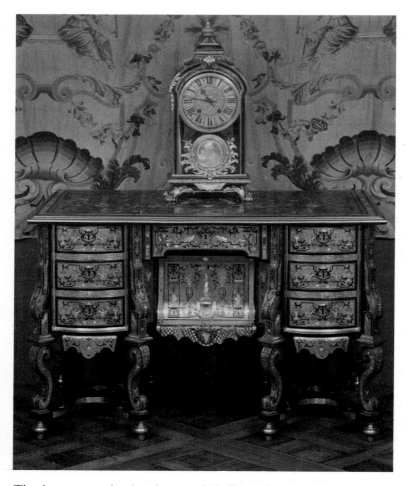

The pine carcase and walnut drawers of this French dressing table, c.1700, are veneered with Boulle marquetry of brass, ebony, ivory, mother-of-pearl and tortoiseshell, with the colour of the last heightened by red and green foil underlay. The eight S-shaped legs are joined by X-shaped stretchers; these serpentine lines were first adopted c.1680. The dressing table is based on a design of the architect and engraver Jean Bérain, whose ideas were to become very popular; it was from Bérain's designs that André-Charles Boulle made many of his finest pieces.
PREVIOUS PAGES *Italian Baroque at its most splendid is seen in this room at Saragna, with its mirrors of Murano glass enclosed in frameworks of* verre églomisé—*glass decorated from behind with arabesque designs of gold and silver foil. The chandelier of partly gilded metal hangs above two elaborately sculptured Siena marble-topped tables and three throne-like chairs upholstered in Lucchesse velvet inset with panels of tapestry. Rooms such as this were typical of the rooms of state in villas and palaces of wealthy families, intended for show rather than comfort.*

In the further pursuit of the new, the best of the Renaissance ideas became exaggerated. Grotesque decoration, so-called because it had been based on paintings discovered in Roman grottoes, was taken up by the sculptors, who interwove the human and animal shapes with tangles of foliage and shells and distorted them into bizarre forms.

The larger pieces of furniture look like whole palaces adorned with

pilasters and twisted columns. The *cassone* gave way to the cupboard and later to the chest of drawers. Console tables, which served a purely decorative purpose, were made and were sometimes surmounted by enormous pier glasses. They had massive marble tops supported by human figures, fauna and *putti* (infant cherubs) among clusters of vegetation and marine life. Cabinets for housing jewels took pride of place in many grand homes and were very colourful pieces. These more than any other furniture serve to accentuate the variations in local styles on the main Baroque theme. Colour was further added by the rich upholstery of silks from Lucca and Genoese velvets on elaborately carved and scrolled chairs, and by the luxurious hangings on walls and beds.

Several new techniques were developed or expanded during this period, to meet the incessant demand for novelty. *Intarsia* inlay (architectural vistas and still-life scenes built up in a mosaic of many different coloured woods) was used to decorate cupboards and other ecclesiastical furniture. The technique spread from Italy to Germany and the Netherlands by the seventeenth century. *Veneering* also became more widely employed. This is the process of applying a thin layer of finely figured wood to a solid carcase, usually of pine or oak. *Marquetry* is the inlay of designs and pictures using contrasting veneers against a plain background. Ivory, tortoiseshell, mother-of-pearl and metals were also used to achieve different effects. *Parquetry* is the setting of contrasting veneers against each other in geometrical patterns, sometimes to form a three-dimensional or *trompe l'oeil* effect with the clever use of different colour and grain.

In *Boulle marquetry* pieces of tortoiseshell and brass are cut with a saw in identical shapes to make a contrasting design. This was developed from an Italian idea by the Frenchman André-Charles Boulle (1642-1732) towards the end of the seventeenth century. Two distinct marquetries can be made by combining the materials in opposite ways: the design of the brass standing out against the tortoiseshell background, or vice versa. The colour of the tortoiseshell was heightened by laying it over slips of red or green foil, and parts of the carcase not covered with marquetry were veneered in toning woods such as purplewoods or ebony. Being of a somewhat fragile nature such pieces are frequently protected at the corners with ormolu mounts. Ormolu is a French speciality and the English word comes from '*bronze dorée d'or moulu*', which means gilt bronze.

An Italian art was that of *pietre dure*, the inlay of hard semiprecious stones such as lapis lazuli, chalcedonies, jasper and agate, ground flat, into a background of contrasting marble. Delicate designs and pictures were produced and highly prized. Table tops and panels were exported to other parts of Europe from Venice and Florence, to be inset into local furniture. Pietre dure was a laborious and costly process, and it was not long before cheaper imitations followed, such as marble mosaics, which were almost as effective. Cheaper still was the process known as *scagliola*, which consisted of a paste made of selenite powder or gypsum. These pastes were used as paints to imitate marble and pietre dure inlay.

Finally, a great deal of effort went into the development of lacquer in Europe. During the seventeenth century, quantities of lacquered cabinets, screens and panels were imported from the Orient via the Dutch East India Company and they attracted high prices. Oriental lacquer is made from the resin of a tree (*Rhus vernicifera*) and the substance is applied to the surface in several layers, each one drying before the next is added. The hard black or red surface was polished and decorations were added in gold leaf. This resin was not available to European craftsmen and alternative methods were tried, though it was not until the eighteenth century that any could rival the Oriental quality. The most widely used alternative consisted of coating the surface of the wood with a mixture of whiting (paste) and size (glue), and then applying many coats of a varnish made of gum-lac, seed-lac or shell-lac, which are different preparations of resin. Then decorations were outlined in gold leaf and the designs built up in gesso (plaster) for a relief effect. John Stalker and George Parker in England published their *Treatise of Japanning and Varnishing* in 1688 and other similar works followed. Whereas Oriental export lacquer on a black or red background was largely confined to cabinets and screens, in Europe it was applied to most varieties of furniture, including musical instrument cases, clock cases, desks and seat furniture. In addition a variety of background colours were produced: apricot, white, blue, green, red, turquoise and more rarely plum.

The new technique spread northwards only slowly. It was Dutch and French Huguenot refugee craftsmen who finally effected the transition from the surviving medieval styles to an English and northern European Baroque. In the north, furniture was still mostly of oak, and local Renaissance interpretations included bulbous bed posts and table legs, while the supports on the other main pieces of furniture, the dresser and the court cupboard, sometimes took the form of lions or goddesses. Only small quantities of inlay, usually boxwood and holly, were used on headboards and court cupboards and these in no way competed with the carved and gilded splendours of contemporary Italy. In England the Baroque never really caught on as it had in southern Europe.

The seventeenth century saw two major advances in timepieces. In 1657 a Dutchman, Christian Huygens, found a way of applying Galileo's pendulum principle to clocks. This improved accuracy to such an extent that for the first time minute hands were added. Secondly, the Englishman Robert Hook invented the anchor escapement, so that clocks could be made to run for longer periods, even up to twelve months. This involved the use of heavier weights, which tended to pull the brackets on which the clocks sat from the walls. So a new branch of cabinet making was needed to produce a clock case capable of supporting the movement and housing the weights. Clocks standing on the floor in these cases are longcase clocks; they are commonly called 'grandfather' clocks, and if under six feet, 'grandmothers'.

Clockmaking continued to flourish in France, Switzerland and Germany, but during the seventeenth century the finest movements were made by English craftsmen, notably Thomas Tompion, Joseph Knibb, William Clement and Daniel Quare.

In the course of the century, the Murano glass factory acquired two major competitors. In Bohemia (now part of Czechoslovakia), the medieval technique of decorating glass on the lapidary's wheel (the lathe used to cut and polish stones) was revived; etching with fluoric acid became possible, and etched and enamelled ruby- and emerald-coloured table glass was made in large quantities to compete with the crystal glass of Murano. This Bohemian glass was hereafter unrivalled in Europe until the 1730s.

The Bohemians also specialized in the technique, which had been practised in Roman times, of etching designs on gold leaf protected between two layers of glass. Most of this type of decoration is on vessels of tumbler shape, sealed at the rim. They also revived the art of cutting glass, known to both Roman and Islamic craftsmen, and the Bohemian cutting machines driven by water power, together with better abrasive and polishing preparations, made the job easier.

Diamond point engraving appears on early Venetian glass, and during the seventeenth century the technique spread to France, Germany and England, where the intricate Italian designs were copied. The Dutch, more resourceful, engraved pictures. They also were the only ones to enjoy success with stippling, a form of diamond point engraving, where dots or short lines are engraved to build up a design.

Murano's other rival was England, for the Dutch engravers preferred English glass. The importance of Venetian table glass declined after an Englishman, George Ravenscroft, had perfected flint glass in 1676. The addition of lead to the glass mixture increased its weight, and also tinged the glass a dusky grey. However, this glass was subject to surface deterioration, although by 1685 a better glass was developed which enabled England to usurp the prominent position so long held by Murano.

Hard-paste porcelain continued to be imported from China and Japan, and Oriental decorative motifs now began to appear on European pottery. In 1602 the first cargoes of Chinese blue and white porcelain arrived at Amsterdam. To start with the Delft potters adopted Chinese designs only on the borders of their plates, retaining their gay polychrome designs in the centres, but soon nearly all delftware was only blue and white. This pottery was made not only in Delft, but all over Holland. Glazing was now applied to the backs as well as to the fronts of pottery in closer imitation of porcelain. For the rest of the century most of the designs were Chinese in derivation, though sometimes combined with borders of Baroque motifs.

Quantities of wall tiles were produced in Holland, at first decorated with fruits, flowers and pomegranates, the emphasis on blue and orange colours. By 1630 the blue and white craze had spread to tiles as well. The most common subjects were people and ships, and most had simple corner motifs. As the century closed, Italy was beginning to produce the first European soft-paste porcelain.

The caudle, or two-handled cup and cover, derives from Germany and became a popular domestic item throughout Europe and America in the 17th and 18th centuries; the line of the bowl and the type of handles vary according to the locality in which the cup was made. Such cups were used to keep a hot bedtime drink from cooling too fast in a chilly bedroom and were filled from a communal pot when the candles were handed round. When removed the cover forms a saucer for the cup. One person's portion was usual, although larger caudles do occur in England. This one, dating from 1660, is of silver-gilt embossed with flowers and has figured handles. It is stamped with the maker's mark GS and a shepherd's crook.

Most of the plate produced in the seventeenth century consisted of new varieties of domestic wares, such as punch bowls, teapots and coffee pots. Declining in use were the great salts, and also ewers and basins to be used at table, since the use of cutlery was becoming more widespread. German pattern books spread the prevailing Baroque designs northwards through the Netherlands to England, but most Continental and English objects were still to be found decorated in local rather than imported styles.

Until the last quarter of the seventeenth century it was Italian craftsmen who generated most of the ideas taken up by the rest of Europe, but for the next hundred years it was France who was to lead the western world in matters of taste.

Left This 17th-century Coromandel lacquer cabinet is mounted on a carved silvered gesso stand, such stands generally being provided for Oriental cabinets on arrival in their country of destination. The Dutch East India Company at Bantam in the Malay Peninsula imported screens and cabinets which were more colourful than those of China and Japan, and though the colours are now somewhat faded, the inside drawers indicate how they once appeared. Because of their bright colours a disconsolate English lacquerer of the time described them as 'the finest hodgpodg and medly of men and trees turned topsie turvie'.

Right A strong contrast is provided by this Flemish cabinet. Apart from the gilt bronze mountings in the architectural centrepiece, the dark wood is left very plain and serves only to frame the paintings on the wings and the drawer-fronts in the style of Sir Peter Paul Rubens (1577-1640), in whose house in Antwerp the cabinet now stands. The centre two panels show Perseus rescuing Andromeda and the other scenes are taken from the familiar legends of Greece and Rome.

Below right Elaborate portable writing boxes, known as *vargueños*, are typical of Spanish furniture in the later 16th and early 17th centuries. They differ from later types in that they have a full front which rests on the sliding pulls of the stand. The rectangular case, often of walnut or chestnut, is divided into drawers around a small centre cupboard, the architectural motifs of which reflect the Renaissance style. These boxes are rarely found on their original stands.

Below Made in southern Germany in the second half of the 17th century, this walnut-veneered marriage cabinet is supported on a solid back and two front legs standing on bun feet. On the central door, below which is a slide, stands the figure of Justice with her scales. It is the fine bloom of these early walnut veneers for which they are sought; unfortunately many pieces have been stripped of this by over-zealous polishers.

Right The ebony frame of this Florentine prie-dieu (praying desk) is inset with medallions of coloured hardstones, and the lower centre panel is composed of *pietre dure* (see p. 30). The lower columns and the pediment reflect the monumental treatment given to Italian furniture in the 17th century.

Opposite above left Carved and gilded armchairs such as this were made in France *c.*1660 during the reign of Louis XIV. Towards the end of the century the tall rectangular back with a straight top gave way to a curved back. The arm rests, which were sometimes upholstered with little elbow pads, are already curved as are the supports. These chairs were sometimes painted red or green and were usually upholstered in velvet, tapestry, damask, or (as here) in brocade, trimmed with a silk or wool fringe.

Opposite above right A small American chest, developed from English Jacobean models, made in the last quarter of the 17th century, possibly by Peter Blin of Wethersfield, Connecticut. The woods are oak, pine and cherry. The top section is a large storage box with a lid. Beneath are three panels carved in low relief with sunflower and tulip motifs. In the centre panel are the initials WSR. Anglo-Flemish medieval and Renaissance styles are reflected in the ebonized split spindle decoration and the turtle-back handles of the drawers.

Opposite below Oystershell patterns in walnut were extremely popular in the 17th century especially in England. They were made up of complete oval sections cut through the branches of small trees. This table, made *c.*1680, with walnut veneer on a beechwood frame, has the oyster sections arranged to make an oval frame on the top. This sets off the predominant decoration of floral marquetry, heightened with leaves of green-stained ivory. The turning of the legs is typical of the period, but more elongated than the Continental equivalent. The marquetry is repeated on the X-shaped stretcher. Its ball feet are of the type most common in the 17th century; they remained in vogue until replaced by the pad foot of the early 18th century.

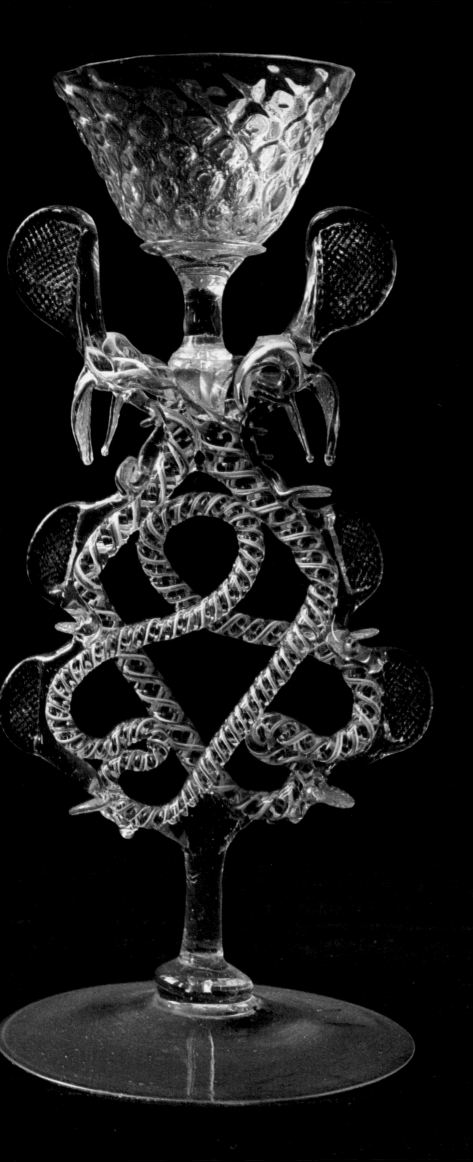

Left 'Winged' glasses were made in Germany and the Netherlands and were copied from similar ones made at Murano. The bowl stands on a tall stem composed of a tortuous arrangement of twisted or clear glass, at the edge of which are impressed ears of clear glass. The ears were sometimes coloured blue, red, green or gold, as were the twisted threads. Glasses of this type, the bowls of which were sometimes engraved and topped with equally complicated covers, are known as *Flügel Gläser* or *verres à la serpent* as well as winged glasses.

Right Watches were sometimes set into flat bun-shaped cases, the convex section housing the movement. They were usually of copper elaborately decorated with enamel and gilt, precious stones and pierced work. This example, made in 1646, is representative of those made at Blois and later Geneva, and was painted either in Paris or Stockholm by the French artist Pierre Signac. The painting on the lid depicts Queen Christina of Sweden as Diana with her hounds in the company of Count Magnus Gabriel de la Gardie, his wife and his sister-in-law. Around the convex section are six medallions inscribed in Latin as are the lid and the clockface.

Below A *latticino* stand for fruit or delicacies dating from the early 17th century. Around the beginning of the 16th century the opaque white glass known as *lattimo* had been developed at Murano, varying in density of whiteness from semi-transparent to milky, for enamelling. Towards the end of the century it became valued for its own qualities rather than solely as a background, since it was found that it could be used to imitate Chinese porcelain. From *lattimo* glass *latticino* designs were developed with fine threads of white glass and clear glass contrasted to form patterns.

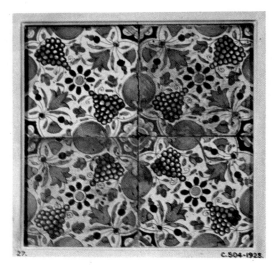

Left Delft tiles were made all over Holland in the 17th century, the idea having emanated from the Arabs in Spain. Tiles made for both wall decoration and floor covering were frequently produced in sets of four, as illustrated here, or as complete pictures involving a large number of tiles. They were made of reddish clay, roughly three-quarters of an inch thick. The dominant blue and orange colour scheme is typical of early delftware.

Right Lions of Buddha, called 'dogs of Fo', are often depicted on Chinese ceramics. These lions bear the mark of the reign of K'ang-hsi (1662-1722) and are of a light, almost sage green. Lions of Buddha were temple guardians and often contain a playful element: in earlier examples the male usually has his paw on a ball. This pair is unusual in that both are playing with cubs.

Below Made in about 1680 in Germany this wine jar is typical of a type of tin-glazed earthenware decorated in imitation of Chinese porcelain that was a speciality of the faience factory at Frankfurt-am-Main. The jar is a faithful copy of Wan-li export wares, painted with Chinese scenes in blue and manganese purple set off against the milky whiteness of the enamel.

Above left Gold cups were made throughout Europe in the early 17th century. This one was produced in Salzburg. Its bowl curves up into a flared lip, and the scrolling handles take the form of elongated female figures. The cup stands on a knopped and stepped trumpet stem, the whole decorated in enamel with emblems and heraldry in the Renaissance style.

Below left The nautilus cup is typical of the elaborate drinking vessels produced by silversmiths in Nuremberg and Augsburg between 1550 and 1650, and is clearly influenced by High Renaissance and Mannerist designs from Italy. The shell was cleaned and ground down until the iridescent mother-of-pearl showed through. It is hinged to the heavy ornate base by four elaborate straps, with the whole of the metalwork intricately and delicately wrought in silver and silver-gilt. The cup was made by Nikolaus Schmidt of Nuremberg in about 1590, and forms part of the table silver at Buckingham Palace.

Right This windmill cup made *c.*1620 is representative of a type known as conviviality cups, produced from the 16th to 19th centuries in Holland. They were generally made entirely of silver, though sometimes the bowl was of glass. When filled with wine the cup was passed around; each drinker would blow into a tiny tube, so turning the sails of the windmill and operating a pointer on a dial. The wine had to be swallowed before the mill had stopped turning, and if the drinker failed he had to drink as many cupfuls of wine as were indicated on the dial. Other such cups celebrated bridals and births.

Below An inkstand made in 1639 bearing the maker's mark AI with a mullet below in a shield. It is in the characteristic style of the van Vianen family of silversmiths. Alternating lions and lionesses form the support, while the candlesticks are held by double figures of *amorini* or cherubs, standing on raised scroll-work plinths. The stand is decorated in repoussé and chased scrollwork with *putti* and figured scenes. In the front is a low central box containing an ink pot with a screw stopper and a pounce pot with detachable top. The end boxes were for wafers. The large box at the back has panels representing the Muses of Music, Arithmetic, Architecture, Astronomy and Literature.

3

From Baroque to Rococo

At the opening of the eighteenth century the social background of the arts was dominated by the aristocracy rather than the courts, and they were supported by an ever-increasing middle class, with money to spend and a desire to 'improve'. It was a period of building and modernization both of town houses and country retreats. There was a trend towards smaller rooms, and these were better adapted to the needs of informal entertaining and conversation, much of which was conducted in the *boudoir* and small salon.

Several styles ran concurrently during this period. Italian craftsmen continued with their Baroque splendours, while Germany created extravagant pieces with exaggerated distortions. The years 1700-30 were transitional in France, during the Régence (1715-23) the heavy *bombé* curves and serpentine lines, though still faintly Baroque, were becoming more delicate and lighter coloured woods were being used. This allowed a freer expression of beauty, leading to the development of the new *Rocaille*, or Rococo, style.

In a more restrained vein, Holland and England, linked by close cultural ties, saw the growth of the William and Mary style, followed by the Queen Anne style, which reflected the quiet taste of the *bourgeoisie*. The main change was from oak to walnut, and most of the furniture, whether seats or cabinets, was made in walnut veneer. The S-shaped legs and bun or ball feet of the William and Mary period were smoothed out into cabriole legs ending in pad or goat's feet, and later the ball-and-claw. Embellishments included feather banding (a fine inlay making a border), shell ornament on the knee of a cabriole, and seaweed or arabesque type marquetry. The use of arrangements of oystershell sections for veneers was developed further, as was that of inlaying floral marquetry on ebony and other backgrounds. Tops of some cabinets were domed, as were the doors and faces of clock cases.

American furniture in the first quarter of the century followed the William and Mary style, using mostly walnut, maple and pine. Inevitably there was a time lag before the designs were generally adopted and in America the styles came into common use after the sovereigns for whom they are named were already dead. American furniture makers also derived from European prototypes pieces of their own, notably the highboy and lowboy, and the butterfly table, so-called because of the shape of the flap supports. Turned legs and bun feet are characteristic of the style, though wing chairs manifest a Baroque influence with their rolled arms and high cresting. Much use was made of painted wood, especially in Windsor chairs, marriage chests and storage cupboards of Dutch derivation.

From about 1725 to 1760 the 'Queen Anne' style dominated American designs. Almost everything stood on a cabriole leg, and the popular shell ornament appeared on the knees of cabrioles and cresting of chairs, and also—in concave form—in the decoration of highboys and lowboys.

The efforts made during the seventeenth century by Louis XIV to found a new national style in France had proved successful. The brilliant team of craftsmen gathered at Versailles embodied the best ideas and techniques in Europe and gave France an undisputed lead not only of fashion but also in quality. The main reason that furniture reached a higher standard in France than elsewhere was the enforced separation of the craftsmen by the guilds. A piece would have to go through the hands of many specialists; the joiner, the veneerer, the polisher, and finally the gilt bronze mount makers. Also called in to add finishing touches might be the lacquerers, the glaziers, and the porcelain plaque makers.

The new style these craftsmen worked in was the Rococo, a refinement of the flamboyant grandeur of the Baroque. Furniture design had by now become a preoccupation of architects, and panelling and sconces, console tables, wall chairs and beds were designed with the house. So the Rococo style is best seen in pieces planned as part of the decor of great houses. It is characterized by a clever interplay of asymmetrical curves, free flowing lines, and curving surfaces, suggesting a continuous flow of movement. Flowers were one of the most popular ornaments, carved singly or in festoons and bouquets on chair crests and seat rails and echoed in the floral marquetry of commodes and cabinets. Furniture was also sometimes painted to match the

pastel colours that had been used to paint the wooden panelling.

Many new pieces of furniture were created to suit the new mood of informality. These included several types of settee and a variety of small tables, each with a special purpose. The style was light and frivolous and readily lent itself to the decoration and design of silver

So-called Amen glasses were made to express loyalty to the Stuart cause, i.e. to the descendants of James II. This trumpet bowl, c.1745, is engraved in diamond point with the Jacobite anthem in full, ending with the word 'Amen'; with the royal crown; the letters IR in cypher, direct and reversed; and the figure 8 on the plain tear drop stem and on the foot. A frequent emblem on Jacobite glass is the rose, representing the crown of England; others are the thistle, the oak leaf and the word 'Fiat'.

PREVIOUS PAGES *With the rapid development of European porcelain there was a short-lived vogue for porcelain rooms. This one, designed for Count Dubsky in Brno in the late 1720s contains a mantelpiece, chandelier, wall brackets, clock and many plaques all made of porcelain. One of those infected by the spirit of competition that fostered the fashion was Madame de Pompadour, who had a summer garden created in the Château de Bellevue of porcelain flowers, all of them perfumed, where she received the King. There are other porcelain rooms still intact in the later Rococo style in Naples and in Spain.*

and porcelain and some clock cases, though glass did not, by its nature, adapt to such variation.

The walnut period in England ended by about 1730 and the years following saw the import of large quantities of dark mahogany from Cuba and Honduras. After some initial reluctance to accept the new style, English craftsmen developed their own version of Rococo, relying initially on Matthias Lock's adaptation of French Rococo motifs to suit the talents of English carvers. Its hardness made mahogany an especially suitable wood in which to carry out Rococo designs, and ornamental motifs such as Chinese figures with lanterns, oriental birds, dragons and lattice work were incorporated into pagoda-type cabinets, seat furniture and tables. The years 1750 to 1760 saw the real flowering of the Rococo in England with new designs by Thomas Chippendale and Thomas Johnson, applying the style to many more types of furniture, including console tables and mirror frames.

The eighteenth century was the great age of European porcelain. The first imitation of Oriental porcelain was a soft-paste variety, made of clay mixed with glass ingredients (known as frit) such as white sand and rock crystal. In England bone ash was also used. In 1709 the secret of true hard-paste porcelain was discovered at Meissen. Since both types were produced in quantity between 1730 and 1800, the collector should learn to distinguish between them. 'Hard' and 'soft' refer to the firing temperature (hard being the higher) and there are three simple methods which serve as a rough guide. To the thumb nail a chip in the porcelain or an unglazed rim will feel like glass if it is hard paste, and like a coarse granular material if soft. Hard paste cannot easily be marked with a pointed object such as a nail file, while soft paste can. Finally, dirt can easily be scrubbed from hard paste but becomes ingrained in the more porous soft paste.

Within a few years many porcelain factories sprang up, and the opportunism of craftsmen helped to spread the secret through Italy, France, Germany, Hungary, Austria and England. Until 1760 the Meissen factory was the most influential. At first porcelain was decorated in the Oriental manner, but gradually a European style evolved, culminating in the *Deutsche Blumen* (German flowers) so much admired and widely imitated. Meissen tableware followed the lines of silver, and porcelain figures replaced those made of wax and sugar, which had been used as table decorations.

At the same time French soft-paste factories were growing in importance, notably Vincennes, which was protected from other French competition by certain privileges concerning loyalty of workmen, imitations and use of gilding. This factory was moved to Sèvres in 1753 and was purchased by King Louis XV in 1759. During the 1740s and 1750s Sèvres porcelains could often be identified by their high-quality gilding, and this, together with the series of background colours developed between 1749 and 1764, enabled Sèvres to compete on an equal footing with Meissen. With the outbreak of the Seven Years War in 1756, the importance of the Meissen factory declined and after that it was to the Sèvres craftsmen that Europe turned for inspiration.

Italian silver in the first half of the eighteenth century was lavishly sculpted and frequently gilded, and this was in startling contrast to the quiet simplicity of silver made in Holland, England, Scotland and America. French silversmiths matched their contemporary cabinet makers in inventiveness and heavy Baroque plate gave way to the lighter Rococo designs, which were suitable for engraving silver. English silversmiths were quicker to adapt to the new fashion than furniture makers, largely because the many Huguenot craftsmen among them were eager to spread the designs of their countrymen. One of these was the brilliant Paul de Lamerie. All through this period, goldsmiths were trying to satisfy the demands of the wealthy in creating every type of watch case, small box and *nécessaire*, and decorating them with enamels, portraits and precious stones.

The years 1700 to 1760 saw many improvements to the mechanics of clocks and watches. A Swiss mathematician, Nicholas Fatio, work-

ing in England with two French clockmakers, learned how to pierce and cut precious stones and to use them as bearings for watch pivots. This resulted in less wear and friction, since the oil was now kept at the pivotal points. The verge escapement was replaced with a variety of others. George Graham, a nephew of the great Thomas Tompion, is credited with the invention of two very simple types, which are still in use today. These are the dead beat escapement incorporated into pendulum clocks, which improved accuracy enough so a second hand could be added; and the cylinder or horizontal escapement which allowed a flatter movement in watches. Further efforts were made to compensate for inaccuracy caused by temperature variations.

Artistically, clock cases kept pace with changing styles. The most ornate were made in France, usually designed as part of a room interior. The austere symmetry of gilt and Boulle-type cases was gradually changed to the eccentric shapes more suited to Rococo decoration. This was most apparent in the cartel clocks, which hung on the wall and whose faces were set in a fanciful arrangement of *putti*, foliage and mythological motifs created in ormolu by such craftsmen as the Caffiéri brothers. Movements were also set into porcelain bodies, or among porcelain figures.

Watches were now carried in the pocket, and an outer case of tooled leather, tortoiseshell, or repoussé gold and silver was necessary

The characteristics of the Queen Anne style can be seen in this settee and two armchairs of walnut veneer, c.1720: in the crested cabriole legs, the shape of the arms, and the ball-and-claw feet. The suite is upholstered in contemporary needlework with figures in cartouches against a background of flowers. The kneehole desk is of walnut and chestnut, also c.1720. The tripod tip-up table is of mahogany, dating from slightly later. The needlework rug was made c.1750 based on a late 17th-century crewelwork design.

for protection. Generally the clocks and watches of France and Switzerland led the field in decoration, while English craftsmen concentrated on improving performance.

The finest glass of this period is undoubtedly English and Irish, although Murano and Bohemia continued the production of their coloured glass. There were two main improvements in the techniques of flint glass production. It was discovered that by being heated to a great temperature and then cooled very slowly, the glass became tougher and less liable to chip or crack. This meant it could be cast more thinly. Secondly, the darkish tint of flint glass was more or less eradicated when the size of the melting pot was increased, so that glass became clearer and more brilliant. Many examples survive, including decanters, chandeliers, dishes and wine glasses. The latter ranged from the sturdy baluster stems cut in low relief, through straight stems containing tear drops, to numerous intricate compositions of air twists, opaque twists and hollow twists.

Left Holkham Hall, Norfolk, was begun in 1734, and was designed in the Palladian style for the Earl of Leicester by his architect friends Robert Earl of Burlington and William Kent. By the 1750s part of it was habitable. In the green state bedroom the four-poster bed and furniture were designed by Kent and the original Genoese velvets have survived.

Below William Kent designed this mahogany kneehole desk around 1730. It has a green leather top, and is decorated with lions' heads and claws with carved borders picked up in gilt. On the desk are a pair of hexagonal *famille rose* vases (Ch'ien-lung, 1736-95) decorated with panels of flowers and land-scapes, the necks adorned with Louis XVI

ormolu scroll handles. Between the vases stands a Chinese porcelain group (K'ang-hsi, 1662-1722) of three dogs supporting a green glazed vase with ormolu mounts of the Louis XV period.

Bottom A small cabinet with nine drawers on a stand decorated with fretwork dating from about 1750; like the pair of sofas it is in the Chinese Chippendale taste. The seats are covered in silk and wool petit-point worked with flowers made in 1765. The latticework on the stretcher and the frieze of the cabinet stand are typical of Chippendale's Chinese designs, as are the pagoda motifs on the sofa splats. Other similar pieces include display cabinets, china tables, hanging shelves and secretaires.

Left The rolltop bureau and similar pieces show the transition from the Louis XV style to that of Louis XVI. Unsigned, it was made *c.*1750. The excesses of the Rococo encouraged a swing back to more classic forms, and here Rococo elements such as the cabriole legs are combined with classical motifs like the inlaid urn and the more restrained ormolu mounts. The chairs are also French, *c.*1770.

Below left Bernard van Risen Burgh made this marble-topped commode with Oriental lacquer panels and delicately twisting gilt bronze Rococo mounts. Many of his pieces bear the stamp B.V.R.B. made with an *estampille*, the ébeniste's mark with which everyone except craftsmen working for royalty were supposed to stamp new and repaired furniture. This piece is similar to van Risen Burgh's earliest documented work, made in 1737 for the French Queen Maria Lesczynska at Fontainebleau.

Above right Pennsylvania's settlers included a large contingent from Germany, who carried with them their goods and chattels in traditional wooden marriage chests. Similar chests were made locally and in New England, and their decoration is frequently based around three arched panels in inlay or, more often, paint. This one, 1700–25, is attributed to Charles Gillam of Old Saybrook, Connecticut, and is made of oak, tulipwood and chestnut painted. In form it is similar to the English mule chest, with its large storage compartment above and long drawer below. The theme of its decoration is possibly of Jacobite inspiration, since it depicts the crowned emblems of England and Scotland united beneath a single crown.

Right Highboys were made in quantity in all thirteen American colonies, and for the whole of the 18th century were the showpieces of American furniture. Lowboys (i.e. dressing tables) were frequently made to match. On this one the legs are turned in the American interpretation of the Baroque, which dates the piece between 1700 and 1720 (though the style is still known as William and Mary), and the stretchers repeat the curves of the skirting. Colour contrasts were a prime form of decoration; this piece is veneered in maple. It was originally owned by the mother of George Washington.

Above left These Vienna baskets are decorated with applied enamelled flowers and have pierced sides and stalk handles. They carry the impressed shield marks on the underside, indicating that the pair was made between 1744 and 1749. The Vienna hard-paste factory was the second to be established in Europe. During its first period, 1719-44, it was run by Claudius Innocentius du Paquier, and used the same clay as Meissen. In 1744 du Paquier sold the factory to the Austrian Empress Maria Theresa; and it was shortly after that that these baskets would have been made.

Below left One of a pair of dishes in the form of vine leaves and painted with flowers. On the underside are the Höchst crown and impressed wheel marks of the period 1750-55. The Höchst factory was situated between Frankfurt and Mainz. The full-blown tulip and other flowers are based on a Meissen design; the brownish border frequently appears on both Continental and English porcelain. Höchst is also famous for its figures, the earliest being Italian comedy models and later the pastoral groups of Johann Friedrich von Lücke.

Opposite above Five of the figures from a Meissen monkey band, which consists of eighteen figures and three music stands. They were probably modelled by Johann Joachim Kändler, who was appointed in 1731 and by 1740 was modelling a vast range of porcelain. His best known tableware is the famous swan service made for Count Brühl, and his figures include characters from Italian comedy, elegant courtiers and their ladies, sportsmen and their companions, peasants, street criers and map sellers. A quite different theme is the monkey band illustrated here. Kändler grew up in the Baroque tradition of early Meissen, and handled the change to Rococo somewhat uneasily, as can be seen in the stands of the musicians.

Opposite Three pieces typical of the 'Chinese' wares produced during the 1730s in the faience factory at Ansbach. Between 1730 and 1760 the factory developed two distinct lines. One involved painting the tin-glazed pottery in underglaze blue, and adding red and gold lacquer in imitation of Japanese Imari ware. The other, as shown here, was copied from the Chinese *famille verte* in the style of K'ang-hsi. The dominant colours, which are thick yet translucent, are deep emerald green and mauve-blue, with accessory colours of yellow, red-brown, olive green and manganese in imitation of the Chinese aubergine.

50

Left The English factory at Stratford-le-Bow, which produced a glassy soft paste, took out a patent in 1744 to 'produce earthenware equal to china or porcelain imported from abroad'. This they did. To the touch, Bow porcelain feels 'soapy'. When held to a bright light the dense milky paste shows translucent crescent shapes. Though it will chip, it rarely cracks. The finest period of all was 1755-59, at the end of which Thomas Frye, who owned the patent, retired. This pair of vases was made in about 1755. They are encrusted with flowers and decorated with butterflies and polka dot circles, the lids topped with birds of prey and the handles in the form of masks.

Below The Italian Capodimonte factory was established by Charles of Bourbon, son of Philip V of Spain. His interest in porcelain is not surprising, as he married the grand-daughter of Augustus II, founder of the German Meissen porcelain factory. The best soft-paste porcelain, which was translucent and pure white, was produced at Capodimonte between the years 1743 and 1759. In 1759 Charles succeeded to the Spanish throne, and the whole factory, including Italian workers, their families and a large quantity of paste, was removed to Spain where it became the Buen Retiro

factory. This plaque is an early Buen Retiro piece, decorated with Chinese figures and made to decorate a *chinoiserie* porcelain room.

Above This beautiful plate comes from a dinner service made by the Sèvres factory for Catherine the Great of Russia (1729-96). The background colour is the famous 'bleu céleste' introduced in 1752. It is often said that the quality of the gilding alone will identify a Sèvres piece; it is applied fairly thickly and is often finely chased. The royal cypher is in the centre, and the trails of flowers, the inset medallions and plaques with mythological scenes are typical of the 1760s.

Above left A Dutch sweetmeat dish, of oval shape, standing on a short stem with a domed foot which reflects the shape of the bowl. On either side are scrolling handles ending in an animal head. One of the indented panels contains an impaled shield inscribed AI 1715, which is surmounted by a coronet enclosed by mantling. Dutch silver was of sterling quality only for the finest pieces; ordinary domestic plate contained nine per cent more copper than sterling.

Below left This heavy English silver cup and cover bears the London mark of 1736-7 (although not that of its maker). It has cast scroll handles, and a leaf which springs from the volute forms the thumb piece. The cup and cover are both decorated with applied cut-card work. This type of cup and cover superseded both the tall elaborate standing cups of the early part of the preceding century and the two-handled caudle cups, posset cups and porringers of the second half of the 17th century.

Opposite Coffee pots came into use around 1650 at the time coffee houses were becoming popular meeting places. Their early form, which lasted until about 1735, was a conical shape tapering upwards, with a domed lid; frequently the spout was set at right angles to the handle. This coffee pot, made by Paul de Lamerie in 1745, shows the later bulbous pear shape that was then appearing on casters and tankards and was much more ornate than its Queen Anne predecessor. De Lamerie, who was of Huguenot descent, was one of the greatest English goldsmiths of the 18th century. He completed his apprenticeship in 1712 and was active until 1751.

Left The habit of taking snuff started in Europe in the 17th century and did not lose favour until about 1850. All but two of the snuffboxes shown here are French. The top one is German, *c.*1750, and its monkey form combines scent bottle and snuffbox. At the bottom left is an extremely rare Russian box, of gold inset with other metals. The others are gold boxes made in Paris in the reign of Louis XV, the earliest (bottom right), inlaid with mother-of-pearl, in 1744, and the latest (bottom), of enamelled gold, in 1764.

Right One of a set of candle sticks made by the French court silversmith Thomas Germain (1673-1748) around 1740. Germain's services were in demand as well by the royal houses of Portugal, Spain and England. He made a great variety of pieces which ranged from toilet sets, furniture, table services, inkstands and chandeliers to ecclesiastical pieces. His stamp consisted of his initials TG with a fleece surmounted by a fleur-de-lys and a crown.

Below Catherine II, who succeeded to the Russian throne when her husband Peter III was murdered by her supporters, owned this magnificent toilet box for travelling. It contains thirty-five pieces of silver-gilt, including candle sticks, drinking vessels, a dish and salver, brushes, mirrors, ointment jars, bottles and many other necessary objects. The case is covered in tooled red morocco leather and is lined with red velvet. It was refurbished for the Grand Duchess Alexandra Nicolayevna, daughter of Nicholas I, on the occasion of her marriage to Friedrich-Wilhelm of Hesse.

Left This portable clock decorated with hunting motifs was made in Dresden, *c*.1720, the works by Gottlieb Graupner and the case by Johann Heinrich Köhler, the court jeweller. The silver-gilt case rests on a base of marble wood supported by couchant lions. The whole is encrusted with diamonds, emeralds and chrysolites, and decorated with green enamel. The scene at the top represents the legend of St Hubert, patron of hunters.
Right The movement of this English clock is by W. Mitchell of East Burnham, and the elegant case of oak decorated with raised gilded gesso on a green lacquer ground was made *c*.1735. The eight-day movement has a brass dial and silvered hour circle, and the days of the month can be seen through a small window concealed by the hour hand. The usual colours for lacquer were red and black, because there was a problem in preventing other colours from turning dingy. This one has been cleaned up, and the original colour shows through in patches.
Far right In the period of the Régence in France (1715-23) longcase clocks were first made smaller and were thus better suited to the smaller informal rooms. The case of this clock which dates from the Louis XV period, is of kingwood and tulip wood with exquisite inlay of realistic foliage in the style of Bernard van Risen Burgh.
Below In the first half of the 18th century the exquisite bronze-working which was applied to wooden furniture was also used to make cases for clocks. This fine example shows the collaboration between the eminent bronzeworker Caffiéri and Baltazar Martinot, one of a family of Parisian clockmakers.

Left It was once remarked that these German *Reichsadler-Humpen* (beakers decorated with the Imperial eagle) should be called fool's glasses, because they hold far too much—generally two or three pints—for any one person to handle. They frequently had the domed covers topped with a finial seen on other wine glasses of the period. This one has a gilded band round the top and is decorated with red, white and blue enamel dots. The mounted horsemen represent the Emperor with the seven electors. The greenish tint of the glass is due to the addition of potash, which contained potassium carbonate, extracted from burning vegetation. In France and Belgium this was known as *verre de fougère* (fern glass) and in Germany it was called *Waldglas* (forest glass).

Right A clock, *c.* 1740, by Godin of Paris, supported by a flower-decked ormolu branch, which springs from a heavy base of Rococo scrollwork. Standing by the clock are two Oriental figures of porcelain, the taller wearing a robe of material similar to that of the harlequin figures made by German and English porcelain factories. The clock face is enamelled, framed in a typically asymmetrical ormolu mount, itself decorated with porcelain flowers.

Below The light baluster knopped stems of these glasses, made in the first half of the 18th century, contain tear drops and the beginnings of air twists, which are derived from the Venetian hollow knop. With flint or lead glass, hollow knops were difficult to reproduce, and air bubbles resulted. It has been suggested that an accidental elongation of a bubble led to the first of the air twists, which were popular between 1740 and 1760. Opaque twists were a Bohemian invention, produced similarly to the Murano threaded glass.

4

Neoclassicism

The last forty years of the eighteenth century encompassed a quick succession of styles, all of them variations of the main Neoclassical theme. The uncertainties and upheavals in France meant that this was a period of standstill for French craftsmen, and new designs came largely from Great Britain and were copied and adapted all over Europe and America.

Furniture continued to be the concern of architects. The first of these to emerge with a Neoclassical style was the Scotsman Robert Adam. His firmly-stated designs provided a welcome contrast to the lively and restless naturalism of the Rococo. They were mostly for side tables, semi-circular commodes, wall chairs and mirrors: the pieces which comprised the fixed interiors of rooms. The decoration was modelled on Roman murals and the effect was both formal and delicate. The curving shapes of the Rococo were replaced by straight ones, and the cabriole legs of chairs and cabinets became either columnar and fluted or square and tapering.

A well-preserved pair of scent bottles made of what is known as Bristol blue glass, dating from 1770; each is painted and gilded with a girl carrying a basket of flowers standing under an apple tree. The screw-on caps are of silver-gilt, with twist decoration and embossed with flowers. For travelling they have their own wooden box covered with green shagreen. In the latter half of the 18th century coloured glass, in red, green and blue, was made in 47 factories in England alone, yet it is the Bristol factory which has since been singled out to give this glass its generic name.

PREVIOUS PAGES *Nostel Priory in Yorkshire is remarkable for a rare combination of talents: the house was designed and decorated by Robert Adam, and Thomas Chippendale, whose father was the estate carpenter, made the furniture. Adam's designs for the interior of the saloon are clearly based on the inspiration he drew from ancient buildings and temples. The commode is attributed to Chippendale himself, the lady's writing table in tulipwood and rosewood is also his work, and probably the picture frames too. The seat furniture is by Chippendale and Haig; the harpsichord is a Kirckman of 1766.*

There was a vogue for gilded and painted furniture, and although dark mahogany was still used for ordinary furniture, the finest pieces were veneered with a satinwood or a lighter, more golden variety of mahogany. Inlay was a major form of decoration, and strings of bell-flowers, medallions, honeysuckle and running scrolls echoed the delicate stucco reliefs derived from ancient buildings. The woods used for inlay formed a subtle contrast with the golden backgrounds and were mostly rosewood (sometimes called kingwood) imported from the

West Indies, and sycamore, known as harewood when stained green. Cross-banding and panels were defined with boxwood and ebony fillets.

The other major form of decoration was carving in low relief on legs of furniture and chair backs, and typical motifs were urns, rams' heads and strings of flowers.

The designs of George Hepplewhite were published posthumously in 1788. He developed the elegant refinement of Robert Adam, but concentrated more on domestic furniture than on the formal grandeur of fine houses. Many of his designs were based on graceful vase shapes, evident in chair backs which were shield-, oval- or heart-shaped, in the doors of secretaires, and in the inlay of table tops and commodes.

A third version of the Neoclassical style was that of Thomas Sheraton, whose designs were published in four parts between 1791 and 1794. He followed in the tradition of Adam and Hepplewhite, but was influenced as well by the richness of the Louis XVI style. Thus we find secretaires and commodes with fluted columns ending in feet that resemble spinning tops, while other pieces such as chests, side tables and sideboards acquired serpentine lines. The furniture was fragile and dainty and many of Sheraton's designs herald the style of the 1800s, based on the Napoleonic 'Egyptomania' craze. By the end of the century other inlay woods were in common use and varied from pale reds to deep browns. These included snakewood, calamander and coromandel from India and Ceylon, partridgewood, purplewood and tulipwood from the Americas, and amboyna from the West Indies.

Though less original than in former times, French furniture was still supplied to most European courts. While the style and shapes were similar to the English, decorative effect relied more on lozenge marquetry and pictorial inlay of vases and bouquets of flowers, this being most apparent in the work of Carlin, Riesener and Oeben. Sèvres porcelain plaques continued to be used as embellishments and these were also exported to other countries and mounted there. Bronze mounts, while still used as decoration, now echoed the Neoclassical motifs and were confined to galleries, borders and corners.

Italian furniture for the great palaces continued in the opulent style of the early eighteenth century, and the finest examples of both interiors and furniture can be seen in the work of Piffetti. In contrast to English and French craftsmen, who revelled in the fine grain and figuring of their medium, Italian cabinet makers disguised their wood in every possible way, with lavish gilding, marquetry and paint. The every-day middle-class furniture is clearly influenced by English designs, though of a shoddier quality.

American furniture, still based on English designs, begins to develop a style of its own. A few craftsmen, notably Thomas Affleck and Ben Randolf, adopted the Rococo styles, and made extravagantly carved mahogany chairs, mirror frames and cabinet furniture. A period of slow development followed the American Revolution, but by 1790 a new Federal style emerged, based on English Neoclassical designs. The twenty-odd years of the Federal period were America's finest for furniture, whose quality of beautiful inlays and fine veneers can compete with the most superlative in Europe.

Porcelain reached its peak in Europe in the closing decades of the eighteenth century, with improved techniques to eliminate firing cracks and other defects. Elaborate dinner services became relatively commonplace, decorated with Neoclassical motifs. Vases acquired graceful lines echoing those depicted in furniture inlay; some were mounted in ormolu in keeping with the general decorative style. The early figures which formed part of a table decoration were made to be viewed from all sides, but later models, made for cabinet displays and mantlepiece garniture, were more often given a plain or leafy back. Porcelain continued to be decorated in enamels and gilding, but a new technique developed and practised mostly in England was that of transfer printing, brought to perfection by the Worcester artist Robert Hancock. New jasper wares came from the English Wedgwood factory and were decorated with cameos inspired by the medallions of the Neoclassical repertoire. Biscuit porcelain figures and groups gained favour and were made in imitation of marble Neoclassical statues. There was much copying of patterns; after the declining influence of Meissen Sèvres designs are reflected, and it often takes a trained eye to sort out originals from copies. Correct allocation of pieces to their factory of origin is judged not only by design, but also by the feel of the paste, its translucent colour and minute details such as the shape of a lip or the thickness of the glaze in a rim.

Most porcelain was marked, but this is often no proof of where a piece was made, because many lesser factories copied more prestigious marks. Sometimes a painter added his own mark. If this appears with that of the factory a more certain attribution can be made. The fact that many pieces were also decorated outside the factory in which they were made adds confusion.

The history of most European porcelain spans only about eighty years. With the industrial revolution of the late eighteenth century and the increasing trend towards machine technology, there was a corresponding decline in the requirement of fine porcelains, and only the Sèvres, Meissen and the Italian Ginori factories on the Continent, and the Worcester and Derby factories in England, were able to adapt to the techniques of mass production.

Silverware from about 1770 acquired regular symmetrical outlines in keeping with the Neoclassical style, and scrolling motifs and delicate fluting were combined with embossed ornament such as acanthus leaves. As in the preceding century, much fine French silver went into the melting pot to finance wars and most of what remains is domestic ware. Happily no such disasters occurred in England, where much of the simple but elegant Georgian silver remains in the homes of English families.

A major development in the silver field was the technique known as Sheffield Plate, invented by Thomas Bolsover. This was a process whereby silver was fused onto a copper body, and factories set up in Sheffield and Birmingham subsequently produced every known variety of plated object. (During the nineteenth century the copper base was gradually replaced by other base alloys of a silvery colour.)

Movements of clocks, while always being improved, had been through their important developments, and this period is remarkable only for the variety of clocks produced. Cases were adapted to the Neoclassical style, becoming lyre-shaped or vase-shaped and embellished with pillars, porcelain, lacquer or bronze. The close collaboration of a wide variety of artists was of more importance here than in any other art form.

The movements of fine watches were also gradually improved in several European centres. England, as before, concentrated on precision, while France and Geneva were more interested in developing new types of timepieces, and making practical additions. Geneva craftsmen were also involved with the crafts of enamelling watch cases, and these were given a translucent coating to protect the painting, and produce a more brilliant finish.

There were no really important new glass-making techniques in the second half of the eighteenth century. Bohemian crystal glass continued to compete with English and Irish flint glass, and though the latter still retained a smoky tint, it was well suited to deep cutting, and widely used for tableware and chandeliers. Production of coloured glass began in England, especially at Nailsea and Bristol, and deep green, blue, purple and red shades were made. A quantity of pinkish tinted opaque glass was made on the Continent and in English factories as well. However, it is the whiteness of Bristol opaque glass that is the quality particularly sought after.

This example of a tambour desk, c.1790, an American speciality, is richly veneered in contrasting satinwood and golden mahogany. The tambour is the sliding reeded front of the upper compartment, which draws back to reveal secretaire compartments. The two slides are separated by a small centre cupboard, which corresponds to the arrangement of the drawers below. Two pull-out slides support an almost flat fall front, which provides a writing surface.

Left The German cabinetmaker J. F. Schwerdfeger made this jewel cabinet in 1787 for Marie Antoinette. The simple mahogany frame holds lavishly decorated Sèvres plaques, mother-of-pearl framed panels of under-glass painting and ormolu mounts by P. P. Thomire. It stands on eight tapering columnar fluted legs in the form of quivers, with sumptuous decoration. The top is surmounted with allegorical bronze figures who once carried the royal crown.

Right The gilded sofa was a popular piece of drawing room furniture throughout the 18th century. It took varying forms: the French Duchesse Brisée, which was a daybed in two or three parts; the tête-à-tête or two-seater; chaises longues; and canapés like the one illustrated here. This is one of a pair derived from the work of Georges Jacob (1739-1814), who executed designs by the great Neoclassical painter Jacques-Louis David. They are probably of English craftsmanship, and are made of gilt pinewood with carved arm supports and legs.

Below right The *bonheur du jour,* first made in France in the mid-18th century, is a small lady's writing table with a set of shelves or cupboards at the back, usually made separately. It was copied in many other countries, adapted to local tastes. This one is of the late 18th century, typically French, standing on cabriole legs veneered in tulip-wood. The top is veneered in lozenge parquetry of exotic woods. The long serpentine drawer and writing slide is surmounted by a removable nest of four drawers, with a small pierced brass gallery.

Below Small tables like this one, made in France by Roger Vandercruse in 1760, were used as a base for candelabra and also served a decorative purpose. They usually contain a small drawer and a lower shelf. The top of this one is inlaid with a Sèvres plaque decorated with a lattice pattern of lozenge shapes, and the wood is painted in *vernis Martin* lacquer to match. The four Martin brothers—Guillaume, Etienne Simon, Robert and Julien—perfected their lacquering technique and took out patents dated 1730 and 1744. Unlike most lacquer specialists they used the technique for a great deal more than the imitation of *chinoiseries.*

Above left The Chinese bedroom in Saltram House, Devon, is a good example of the way *chinoiserie* decoration could be adapted to blend with English Georgian architecture. The walls are painted in the Chinese manner. The high bed of golden mahogany is based on a design from Chippendale's influential pattern book, *The Gentleman and Cabinet-Maker's Director* (1754-62). There are also two Chippendale chairs in the Chinese taste. On the carved and painted chimney piece are three porcelain vases flanked by dogs of Fo, all Chinese porcelain made for the European market. The painted mirror picture is also typical of Chinese export wares, though the frames are English.

Below left One of a pair of satinwood console tables with elaborate marquetry and ormolu mounts, attributed to Chippendale. On the table stands a pair of Chelsea oval baskets with pierced sides, painted with delicate sprays of flowers, *c.*1760. These baskets were produced at several factories and are highly desirable as collector's pieces. The Chelsea soft-paste factory was set up in 1743 by the French Huguenot silversmith Nicholas Sprimont and was run by him, with a short interruption, until 1770. The factory's porcelain was later known as Chelsea-Derby, after the amalgamation of the Chelsea and Derby factories.

Right A secretaire bookcase of satinwood veneer dating from about 1775. On the secretaire drawer is a painted panel in the style of Angelica Kauffmann, and the piece combines decoration in paint and inlay. The marquetry of baskets of flowers, classical urns, ribbons and foliage is exceptionally fine.

Below George Hepplewhite published the design for the Pembroke table in his *Cabinet-Maker and Upholsterer's Guide* of 1788; the piece, which consists of a central section with two side flaps supported on wooden brackets, takes its name, according to Thomas Sheraton, from Lady Pembroke, who first ordered it. The finest ones were of satinwood, either inlaid with Adam-type designs or painted in a similar manner. This inlaid Pembroke, with designs clearly inspired by Adam, is of satinwood and stands on an early 18th-century needlework rug.

Above It was from the side table flanked by
urns standing on columns or pedestals, as
used by Robert Adam, that George Hepplewhite derived the sideboard, which
comprises two cupboards and usually a
centre drawer. The left-hand one contained
a cellarette and the right-hand one was lined
with sheet iron and equipped with a tray for
plates and a spirit lamp. This one, probably
made in Baltimore between 1790 and 1800,
is based on a Hepplewhite design. Its fine
mahogany veneer has beautiful inlay.

Left A fine breakfront bookcase representative
of the type made in Charleston, South
Carolina, from English prototypes. It was
produced during the first half of the Federal
period, 1790-1800. The decoration relies on
clever use of contrasting veneers and fine
fillets of inlay. This type of furniture was
invariably made in separate parts, with
handles on both sections to facilitate
movement. The serpentine form of the lower
portion is probably an adaption of the Dutch
mid-18th-century *bombé* line, which appeared
in several areas in America around this time.

Right Semi-circular commodes were
introduced by Robert Adam. This example,
although unattributed, is similar to several
made by the firm Ince and Mayhew around
1770. The background is satinwood veneer,
the centre oval panels are mulberry and
the inlay is of kingwood, harewood and
fruitwood with designs in the classical style.
The legs are typically French in inspiration.

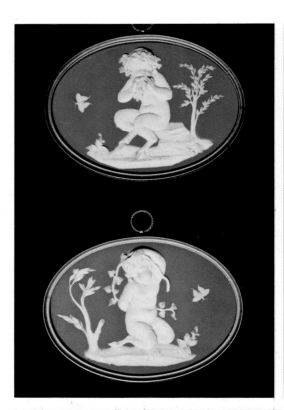

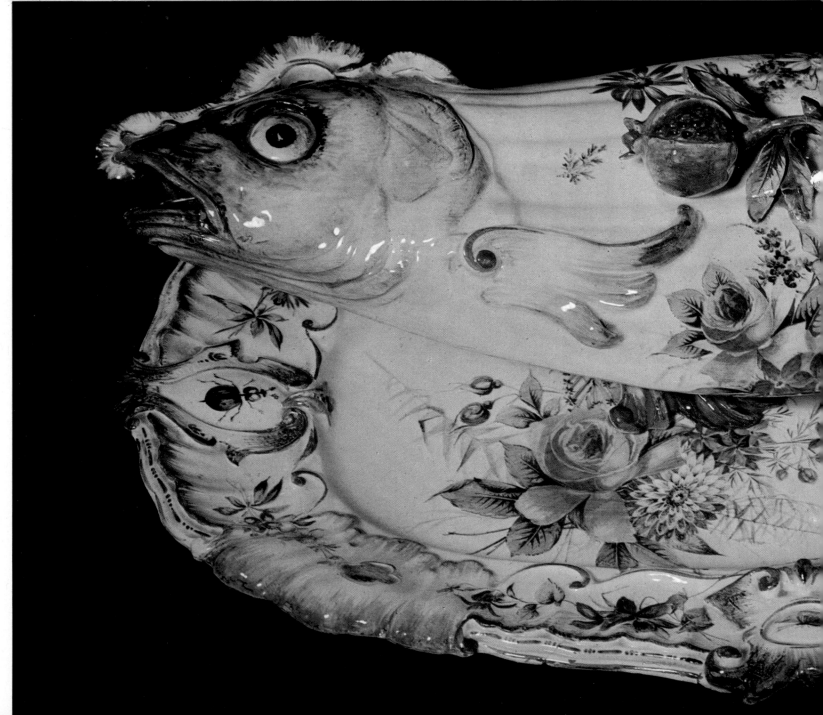

Opposite above left Perhaps Josiah Wedgwood's greatest contribution to English pottery was his jasper ware—a fine-grained stoneware coloured by different metallic stains. He quickly adapted to the Neoclassical taste of the 1760s and by the mid-1770s was using jasper ware to imitate the cameos of Antiquity. These oval medallions of *putti* are typical of Wedgwood's work, and his factory produced vases, cameos, medallions, plaques and mounts in black, blue and sage green.

Opposite above right Soft-paste porcelain was produced at Mennecy from 1748 to 1773, when the factory was moved to Bourg-la-Reine; it closed in 1806. Because of the monopolies favouring the Vincennes/Sèvres factory, Mennecy was not allowed to use gilding. The products were simple, with only a few shapes made in a milky white paste; the decorations were mostly based on Meissen flower paintings. Some of the figures are similar to those produced at Bow during the same period. Mennecy made many little snuff boxes, scent bottles, knife and umbrella handles and toilet pots like these. Charac-

teristic colours are bright blue, rose pink and brownish-green.

Right This pail, or jardinière, from the Tournai factory in Belgium, is decorated with panels of birds from Buffon's *Natural History*, butterflies, insects and centurion heads in *grisaille* on white backgrounds. These contrast vividly with the blue panels, which are similar to the Sèvres 'bleu du Roi'. It is one of a pair, probably from a service ordered by Philippe, Duc d'Orléans, in 1787. Many English artists were employed at Tournai, and much of the porcelain of the 1760s is similar to that produced in the English Worcester and Derby factories.

Below The Nove factory at Le Nove di Bassano near Venice was founded in 1728 and during its early years produced some lovely pieces of porcelain based on contemporary silver shapes, including teapots with Rococo handles, tea bowls and saucers, decorated with scenes, figures and flowers. Later, fish tureens like this one, decorated in fresh colours with sprays of flowers, fruit, and butterflies, were also made there.

Left Tea was on sale in London by the mid-1660s, and large kettles for replenishing the teapot came into vogue during the 18th century, set on stands containing warming equipment. This tea kettle, which is now in Buckingham Palace, was made by Thomas Heming in 1761. Of silver-gilt, engraved with a crown and the initials CR, it was presumably made to celebrate the marriage in that year of King George III to Charlotte-Sophia of Mecklenburg-Strelitz.

Above right Paul Revere (1735-1818) is perhaps the best known of the great American silversmiths and his career spanned over fifty years. He specialized first in the Rococo, and later the classical style. Revere was of Huguenot descent, the son of Apollos Rivoire, also a silversmith. Apart from producing fine silver Paul Revere was a great revolutionary patriot, practised dentistry (then an allied branch of goldsmiths) and in addition he was a highly skilled engraver whose range included the design of banknotes, political cartoons and pictures. This tea service was made in 1792/3, and is in the pure Neoclassical style. Revere stamped his silver with the name Revere in a rectangle.

Right The table and chairs of this dining table setting, from the first decade of the 19th century, are of dark mahogany in the Chippendale manner. The table is laid with the Onslow family's Worcester dinner service, each place setting accompanied by two glasses. The gilded ones are of a type generally imported from Bohemia and the others are a selection of late 18th-century glasses with opaque twist stems. A pair of candelabra of Sheffield plate provide the lighting and the centrepiece is of English lead glass sweetmeat jars and covers.

Below Although, generally speaking, glassware was not affected by sudden changes in fashion, chandeliers tended to follow new styles. This one is similar to many produced to blend with the furniture of the Adam period. Made of English flint glass *c.*1775, the style is manifested in the swags of drops and cascades, the urn-shaped central column and the graceful curves of the arms supporting the candles. The chain holding the chandelier was covered, as was the fashion, with a satin sleeve to suit the colour scheme of the room.

Left During the revolutionary period in France (1792-99) an attempt was made to replace the Gregorian calendar by a 'Republican' one, with twelve 30-day months, five named holidays and a sixth every fourth year to be called Revolution Day to make up the year. The day was to be divided into twenty decimal hours; consequently we occasionally find clocks and watches with dials counting 10 to 100, sometimes with a normal dial as well. An example is this repeating watch, decorated with French allegorical figures, that chimes the quarter-hours. In 1806 Napoleon abolished the new calendar.

Right An American longcase clock dated 1790; this example was made by two of America's greatest experts. The works and chime were assembled by the Huguenot Isaac Brokaw (1746-1826) who signed the dial. The case was made by Matthew Edgerton (1739-1802) of New Brunswick, whose son and namesake carried on the business. Many of their pieces survive. This mahogany case with its heavy carved work is closer to the style of the mid-18th century than to the finer inlaid work of the Federal period. It carries a broken scroll pediment and finial, turned pillar supports, quarter columns on the body and chamfered corners on the base.

Below Made by Chapman of London in 1781, this is a typical matching watch and chatelaine. These useful and ornamental ensembles that dangled from the belt were usually made of silver, pinchbeck (an alloy of copper and zinc used as imitation gold) or gilt metal. Sometimes chatelaines were used to hold not watches but keys, seals or little cases containing scissors, needles, pencils, thimbles and the like. This example carries a watch, a watch key and a seal, and has two other rings on which to attach other *nécessaires*. Four miniature pictures are set off against vivid red enamel backgrounds and framed in borders of seed pearls.

In the early nineteenth century France, though still leading European fashions, was recovering from the aftermath of revolution and the upheaval it had caused. The guilds had been supressed in 1791 and this left the various branches of craftsmen free to join forces under one roof, enabling them to compete on a commercial basis hitherto impossible, and to supply a wider (if less discerning) clientèle. The periods of Napoleon's Consulate (1799-1804) and his Empire (1804-15) were in fact a particularly fertile period for the arts.

In the past there had generally been a considerable lapse of time before new styles became widely known and adopted, but the styles of Napoleonic France were taken up nearly everywhere with unprecedented speed. This was in part due to nepotism: Napeoeon's relations occupied various thrones and embassies of the satelite states of the French Empire, but, in addition, England, Russia, Austria and America all followed suit, as what has been called a 'natural consequence of the superiority of French art'.

The Empire style was stimulated by the French campaign in Egypt and a growing interest in all archeological discoveries—Egyptian, Pompeian, Roman and ancient Greek. The emphasis was on archeological accuracy and purity of form, and the effect tended to be austere. As at other times, the new style was most apparent in the furniture. Marquetry and parquetry, so popular in the eighteenth century, were rejected, and large areas of dark mahogany and rosewood veneers were preferred, enhanced no longer by lavish ormolu mounts but rather by restrained bronze decorations in classical motifs, which were confined to limited areas. Brass inlay, first pioneered by Boulle, was revived and applied extensively, sometimes over large areas; and pierced brass galleries (small raised borders) and brass grilles, used in cupboard doors, were introduced. Black and gold furniture was in vogue, particularly chairs and occasional furniture such as washstands and tripod tables. The curving shapes of the eighteenth century were abandoned in favour of straight lines on cabinets and

commodes, console tables and chiffoniers. Mirrors were used extensively to make rooms look larger. Chaises longues and chairs acquired scrolled ends and sabre legs, and curving X-shaped stool supports were repeated on writing tables. Beds were placed alongside the wall and surmounted by enormous crested canopies. Small dining tables were now circular, frequently resting on a centre column and triangular pedestal, and fall-front secretaires regained favour. Supports were decorated with lions' heads and claws, winged eagles and Egyptian torsos terminating in animal legs, as well as with columns and balustrades.

The French Empire style spread rapidly all over Europe. In England the designs of Sheraton bridged the gap between the Classicism of Adam and the new Empire. These designs were modified by Thomas Hope, whose publication in 1807 (*Household Furniture & Interior Decoration*), though influenced by the great French architect

PREVIOUS PAGES *The interior decoration of Malmaison, Napoleon's country retreat acquired in 1799 by the Empress Josephine, was begun in 1800 by Percier and Fontaine, who worked in the pure classical tradition and were later employed at the Louvre and the Tuileries. This is the library, which reflects the Napoleonic conception of grandeur, combining the elegance that befitted a leader of France with a simple style suited to a military empire. The columns and panelling are of polished mahogany, relieved only by the restrained ormolu mounts on the frieze. The chairs are in the Consulate style, and their square scrolling backs and straight legs are decorated with winged Egyptian busts in characteristic head-dress, the feet being lions' paws.*

In the 19th century mantle clocks, formerly a luxury, became commonplace. This example is French, c. 1810-30, made of ormolu, and the clock is surmounted by an allegorical figure of music, strumming a lyre. An unusual feature of this clock is its silk suspended pendulum. Though unsigned, it is in the Empire style, the decoration on the base is centred on a medallion, and the fact that it is both rectangular and symmetrical reflects the lines of contemporary furniture.

Charles Percier, contained designs strictly based on classical prototypes, and these formed the basis of the English Regency style.

The leading American cabinet maker was the Scotsman Duncan Phyfe (1768-1854) who was joined after the American Revolution by French immigrant craftsmen. Among these was Charles-Honoré Lannuier (1779-1819), who arrived in 1803 and introduced the French style; he was also responsible for the import of large quantities of French ormolu mounts, until then unknown on American furniture.

Each country developed its own specialities: Germany favoured lyre-shaped cabinets and round secretaires resembling Classical temples; a typically English piece was the sofa table, and in America the tambour desk retained popularity.

The brief revival of the arts was unfortunately short-lived, for mechanization was accelerating, increasingly geared to mass production. Royal and wealthy patronage declined, and a desire for cheaper goods brought a lowering in the standard of craftsmanship, as the market for quality pieces lessened.

This decline is most evident in the field of pottery and porcelain. By the turn of the century many of the European and English porcelain factories had gone out of business; only a few were able to adapt to changing conditions. The Welsh factories at Nantgarw and Swansea enjoyed popularity when for a time their products were in great demand due to the shortage of French porcelains. Much of it was decorated in London in the Sèvres style, and it is considered to be among the most beautiful ever produced.

Bone china, made by adding bone ash to the paste, became the standard body for table wares, and at first they were decorated in the Neoclassical manner, though by the end of the period there were signs of a Rococo revival. Jasper wares continued to be produced in the same way as in the eighteenth century, with decoration adapted to the changing taste. Transfer-printed wares from factories such as Wedgwood and Spode became popular, as did the many types of creamware that flooded the market. The Masons' factory developed a new type of stoneware called Ironstone china. The industry which had supplied a wealthy élite was fast changing over to mass production.

Trade blockades with England and France led America to develop her wide range of stonewares; the first really successful porcelain enterprise was that of the Tucker family, during the years 1826 to 1838. Towards the end of this period the Tucker vases, decorated and gilded in the Sèvres manner, reached a standard comparable to European porcelain. Thereafter, American porcelain factories were almost entirely devoted to commercial production.

Glassmakers too were affected by industrialization. One-, two- and three-piece moulds were developed, into which the glass was blown and pressed either manually or mechanically, a plunger forcing the glass into all parts of the mould and impressing its pattern. By the 1830s the method was widely used and the new technique made possible new shapes and designs at more acceptable prices.

The style of the silver in this period reflects that of the Empire, drawing on decoration from Greece, Egypt and Imperial Rome. Two types of plate predominated: on the one hand, important commemorative pieces were made to honour the feats of Napoleon, Wellington and others; on the other, cutlery, candelabra and the like were produced for the mass market. In 1805 the foundations were laid for a new process called electro-plating, in which electrical currents are used to deposit silver on a base metal. Sheets were coated on both sides and sold to silversmiths to make up into individual pieces.

Finally, a word about collecting. Since anything thought to be 'good' will have enjoyed the attentions of experienced copiers, it is advisable before one starts to collect antiques to acquire some knowledge of the subject. Collectors of silver should beware of three pitfalls. First: only British silver has been hallmarked by law from an early date; Continental silver, especially that of Germany, generally contains a higher proportion of base alloy. Second: a piece may have been altered, such as a sugar caster later changed to a cream jug with decorations added. Third: genuine marks from old pieces have been discovered fused on to later ones to give them a higher value.

Ceramics have always been copied, from the T'ang figures onwards, and to sort these out calls for specialist knowledge. Much of the output of the Sampson factory in Paris in the second half of the last century consisted of reproductions of eighteenth-century and Chinese armorial porcelains (i.e. made for the European market and decorated with purchaser's arms) but it is often signed and should usually be quite obvious to the discerning eye. Sampson also speci-

One of a set of American cane-seated chairs (of which nine survived) in the Empire style c.1820, attributed to John and Hugh Findlay, who worked in Baltimore, Maryland, in the first half of the 19th century. Of painted maplewood, they are based on the Roman version of the Greek klismos, a chair with sabre legs back and front. Each of the nine chairs is painted individually. A similar set was designed for the White House by the architect Benjamin Latrobe for America's fourth president James Madison.

alized in reproducing 'Delft' wares. One must bear in mind, also, that porcelain and pottery can now be mended so finely that damage is virtually invisible except in a strong light. The coloured glass wares produced in England in the eighteenth century have been expertly imitated in Czechoslovakia and these copies are very difficult to spot.

Throughout the nineteenth century furniture was painstakingly copied, though the woods and method of construction were not always closely followed. In addition, of the many pieces that were constructed in two parts—such as highboys, two-tiered chests of drawers, and chests on stands—some became separated and remarried to new partners later, or had the missing piece 'made up'. The type and condition of the brasswork is often a reliable indication, but the age or condition of wood can be misleading. For instance, a decline in the popularity of wardrobes has released a quantity of period wood to be made into other things or used for conversion jobs, and a two-tiered chest of drawers might be made into a secretaire bookcase or two small chests, or used for re-veneering broken woodwork, such as chair legs. Furniture is sometimes sold as more or less 'right' by dealers and will fool ignorant buyers. The motto 'Fortune favours the informed mind' is nowhere more applicable than in the world of antiques.

Left This detail is from a French Empire cabinet made by Jacob Desmalter *c.*1810. Furniture makers were now assisted by technical innovations such as the mechanically operated saw, and one consequence of this was that marquetry, so popular throughout the 18th century, was replaced by large areas of figured veneer. In France, Napoleon's European blockade encouraged craftsmen to use native woods such as maple, fruit woods, walnut and elm, but this fine piece is veneered with red bird's-eye mahogany (*acajou moucheté*), the markings and texture being ideal to accentuate the vast range of gilded bronze mounts by Thomire, which are enhanced by mother-of-pearl insets.

Below An English writing table designed *c.*1800. It is based on a design popular in both England and America, incorporating elements of Sheraton and French Empire styles. The table is of fine rosewood veneer and contains two long drawers in the top, framed with brass beading which is repeated in the side panels. The leather surface is surrounded by a brass band. This is surmounted on three sides by a pierced brass gallery designed to keep pens and papers from falling off. The ebonized curving X-frame supports ending in lion masks and carved paw feet are inspired by Roman prototypes, and are joined by a carved rosewood stretcher. The lions' heads recur on the ringed brass handles; this feature is typical of the late Empire phase.

Bottom This heavy mahogany sideboard is typical of the English version of the Egyptian revival. It was made about 1820, and the white and gilt dinner service was made in the Worcester factory at the same time. Below are wine coolers which show up the contrast between the darker mahogany from Cuba, San Domingo and Puerto Rico, and the more golden variety from Honduras. The sideboard stands on a peculiar arrangement of eight twisted columns ending in lions' paw feet and surmounted by masks carved in relief. An unusual feature is the massive back, so popular in Victorian times, with its rope-like border and oblong patera.

Left In the early French Empire style, this little table, which contains small drawers with brass mounts, and is decorated with miniatures of the Napoleonic royal family of Naples, was made in the first decade of the 19th century. The central support is of carved wood, the branches caught halfway up in a band of gilded acanthus leaves, springing from a square band decorated with gilded paterae. The base, like the top, is of mahogany veneer, and stands on the brass lions' paws typical of the Empire style.

Right This Austrian sofa is very much in the German Biedermeier style, and was made probably in Vienna *c.*1820, from the factory of Joseph Danhauser. It is of fruitwood, the figuring and colour of which are pleasing, but it seems unnecessarily adorned with brass finials and the ebony and gilt arm supports like those found on French sofas. High-backed rectangular sofas were made in great numbers, their simple contours and plain surfaces being well suited to the severe and unostentatious style. They usually stood on sabre legs.

Below right The style that emerged in Germany after the stark quality of German Empire furniture was still plain but less austere, and was known as Biedermeier. Characteristic features were plain mahogany surfaces, limited use of gilt bronze mounts, and emphasis on comfort and practicality rather than splendour and decoration. This small oval mahogany sewing table fulfils all the requirements, but the lyre-shaped supports indicate that the style still derives from the classical prototypes. Unhappily, the quiet and solid simplicity of the Biedermeier period was short-lived.

Left An American mahogany breakfront secretaire probably made in Salem between 1780 and 1805. There were a number of cabinet makers in the area producing secretaires based on English designs. The urn-shaped finials, strings of inlaid bell flowers, panels of contrasting veneer and border fillets of boxwood are typical motifs, but the legs are distinctly American. These secretaires were sometimes sent to the West Indies on merchant ships to be traded for local products such as rum, sugar and spices which could then be profitably disposed of in New England.

Above right The French immigrant Charles-Honoré Lannuier made this American card table about 1815. As he had been trained in Paris, his first pieces were in the Revolutionary style; he later turned to Empire, and this table, made for the Baltimore merchant James Bosley, contains elements of both. The winged caryatid (female figure who serves as table support), colonnettes and hocked legs are painted black and partly gilt. Round the edge of the folding top of bird's-eye maple are inlaid brass stars, circles and anthemia. The inside of the top is veneered with satinwood.

Below right The Philadelphia workshop of Antoine Gabriel Quervelle (1789-1856) produced this circular mahogany pedestal table in the heavy Regency style, *c.* 1830. Typical of his work is the gilt brass foliate banding on the under edge of the drum, the depressed marble centre, the heavy triangular base standing on carved paw feet, and the gadrooning, which is an ornamental edge of inverted fluting. The table top is of inlaid marble surrounded by a border of stencilled gilt patterns repeated on the base. The feet are painted to resemble *verd antique*, the green encrustation on ancient coins and metals.

Above and below left Like furniture designers, porcelain makers were concerned with imitating the forms of Classical antiquity. This cup, saucer and jug are typical of the hard-paste enamels of the Vienna factory at the beginning of the 19th century, and reflect the extravagant taste of the era. The ground is entirely covered by gold, finely tooled, with delicate miniature painting. These examples carry the underglaze shield in blue of the Vienna factory together with a serial number 803, i.e. 1803; later copies usually did not have the date number and the quality of the gilding is always inferior.

Far left William Ellis Tucker, one of the first successful porcelain makers in America, was born into a family of wealthy Quakers. He was joined in 1826 by his younger brother Thomas, and the factories of the brothers Tucker continued until 1838. The porcelains they produced were much admired; distinctive features are the rich use of gilding and the enamel paintings based on those of Sèvres. The poorly moulded handles on this vase were later improved in the finest Tucker pieces, which, like French porcelain vases, were enhanced with ormolu mounts.

Below left This lovely tureen and stand was made and probably decorated at the Welsh factory at Nantgarw set up by the craftsman William Billingsey. Having been employed at the porcelain factories of Worcester, Derby and Pinxton, he was eager to capitalize on a fine-quality, translucent and soft paste. With government help, he and his son-in-law Samuel Walker started factories first at Nantgarw and then at Swansea. Various factors contributed towards a general shortage of fine porcelain from France, and these two factories enjoyed brief glory, producing porcelain richly gilded and painted with naturalistic flowers. White wares were also sent to London for decoration. The business was sold to Coalport in 1822.

Right The early 19th century marks the beginning of a period of commercialism in the pottery field. The Staffordshire potters were among the first to exploit the ready market. Among many lines, they produced stoneware figures of well-known public personalities, as well as of cricketers, boxers and the like, which sold for a few shillings. This one represents Napoleon Bonaparte in his favourite uniform and characteristic three-cornered hat. Although not fine, these figures are now widely collected.

Napoleon Buonaparte,

Left Several types of glass table sets were popular in the late 18th and early 19th century, and silver or Sheffield plate holders were designed to facilitate the handling of them. Some holders took the form of carriages on wheels, while others were surmounted by a substantial ring to pick them up and pass them. This Sheffield plate holder bears a rare hallmark for 1800. The decanter type vessels are contemporary, the ball-shaped stoppers being less common than those of mushroom design around this period. The moulded and pressed containers carry silver labels reading 'cayon', 'lemon' and 'elder'.

Below Flint glass lustres were used a great deal for both table and mantelpiece decoration. This English pair was made *c*.1825. Each has twelve drops which hang from an upturned saucer, made up of simulated leaves, which are repeated on the candle holder and the foot. The heavy bulbous stem, saucer and holder would have been pressed in a mould. The drops were easily lost or broken and consequently these lustres are frequently amalgamated from several incomplete sets. Nowadays these candle holders are frequently converted for electricity.

Above An American opalescent pressed glass sauce dish of a type made in large quantities between 1825 and 1840. Bakewell's factory in Pittsburg, which had been set up in 1808, was in 1825 the first to patent a mechanical pressing process for glass. This involves forcing glass in its molten state under pressure into a mould. After pressing, the article was polished so that it looked as if it had been cut. The glass industry derived considerable impetus from the new technique, since the much-admired English and Irish cut glass could be copied with some accuracy at a fraction of the cost.

Above left This silver teapot comes from a five-piece service comprising teapot, hot water jug, coffee pot, lidded sugar bowl, and milk jug, made by the American silversmith Samuel Kirk in 1828. He worked in Baltimore, where, in an attempt to emulate the British hallmarking system, silversmiths were compelled to mark their wares with their initials or marks, as well as date letters. Unhappily this lasted only about sixteen years, and the practice was discontinued in 1830. After that date marking was not compulsory. During the post-Federal period there was a vogue for all-over embossing and for rectangular handles.

Below left Around the turn of the century silver-gilt was more popular in France and Holland than in England and America. This little cream jug, about seven inches high, made in Paris in 1800, is a perfect example of the elegant unfussy lines of the French Empire style. It is basically urn-shaped with a handle of simulated rope, and the decoration is of flat chased leaves and honeysuckle. Under the wide pouring lip is an escutcheon in which is engraved the letter C.

Right In the 17th, 18th and 19th centuries miniature boxes, sometimes called portrait boxes, were made for carrying snuff or pills and the like. They were made from gold or silver bases, on to which the decoration was fused. These 19th-century examples show Napoleon Bonaparte (*top left and below right*) and his family. In 1796, aged 29, he married Josephine (*top right*), widow of the Viscomte de Beauharnais, who had been guillotined during the reign of terror. She failed to produce an heir and he divorced her in 1809. The following year he married Marie Louise (*below left*), Archduchess of Austria, who bore him a son, the King of Rome (*centre*), in 1811. Napoleon's personal emblem, the busy bee, is depicted in the enamel border of the oval box (*top left*) and in diamonds on the circular gold box.

Below In 1819 Paul Storr made this sauce tureen and cover, which, as was usual, is a miniature version of a soup tureen. The rather florid style represents a breakaway from the Adam forms which had influenced silversmiths until the turn of the century. The oblong fluted bowl has heavy scrolled feet and is adorned with a massive pattern of oak leaves repeated on the rim, handle and base. Paul Storr was working in London between 1792 and 1821.

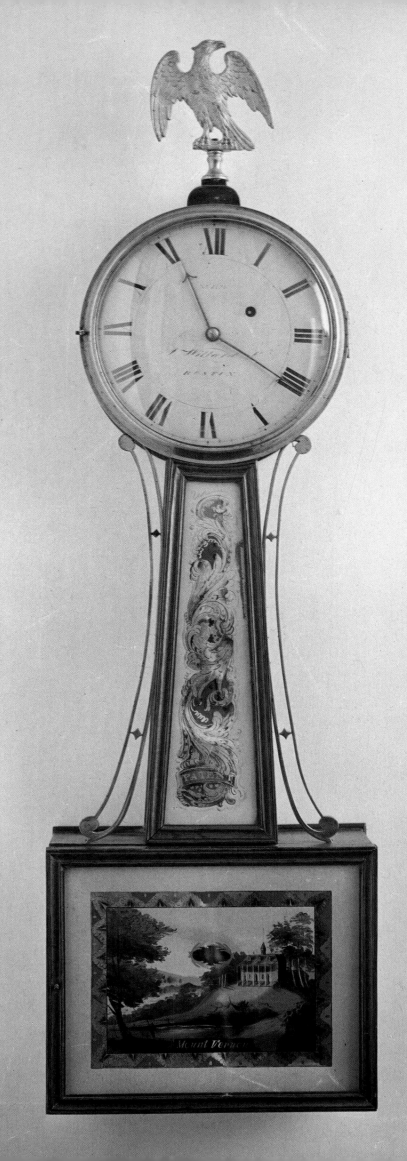

Right Simon Willard, one of four brothers working in and around Boston in the Federal period, first patented the banjo clock in 1802 as an 'Improved Timepiece'. This example was made some thirty years later by his nephew, Aron Willard Junior. There were many varieties of banjo clock, some with alarms and chimes, and their design was an original and specifically American contribution to clock case design. They had brass eight-day movements, and were the American version of the European cartel, or wall clock. This one, topped by the American Eagle is decorated, like many American clocks, with an under-glass painting of a well-known architectural vista. Because of their popularity, these clocks continued to be made throughout the 19th century.

Below In 1797, an Act of Parliament required a levy of five shillings per annum to be paid on all clocks and watches. Since many people promptly sold theirs, many inns and taverns installed clocks, and these became known as Act of Parliament clocks. Characteristic features were large unprotected round or octagonal wooden faces, two or three feet in diameter, with short black trunks, which were sometimes also lacquered. The numerals and other gilding are now frequently obscured by a layer of carbon, due to the smoky atmosphere of these public places. The shape was retained long after the Act was repealed in 1798; this clock was made *c.*1810.

Index

Acknowledgments

The author would like to thank Michael Raeburn for his assistance in the preparation of this book.

The publishers are grateful to Brian Mayers Associates for designing this book.

The publishers would like to thank the owners, authorities and trustees of the following collections and museums for their kind permission to reproduce the illustrations in this book:

American Museum at Bath: 35 above right, 88 above left, 94 right
Ashmolean Museum: 44
British Museum: 14-15, 17, 27 right
Brooklyn Museum: 92 above
Burrell Collection, Glasgow (photos M. Dyer Associates): 1, 13 both, 15 above, 21 above and below left, 26, 54 above
Charleston, S. C. Museum, exhibited in the Heyward-Washington House: 70 (Helga Studio photo courtesy Magazine ANTIQUES)
Christies: 16 below, 40 right, 41, 56, 80
Collection of the Newark Museum, New Jersey: 77 right
Collection of William Nathaniel Banks: 87 above (Helga Studio photo)
Connaissance des Arts: endpapers (photo J. Guillot), 4-5

(photo R. Guillemot), 5 (photo J. Guillot), 27 left (photo R. Guillemot), 46-47 (photo R. Guillemot), 57 left (photo R. Guillemot), 59 left (photo R. Guillemot), 66 (photo R. Bonnefoy), 76 (photo J. Guillot), 93 (photo R. Guillemot)
Constance Chiswell Collection: 38 below (photo M. Dyer Associates)
Cooper-Bridgeman Library: 23 below, 24 above and below, 31, 48 below, 55, 61, 64, 84, 89, 90-91, 92 below left and right
Diplomatic Reception Rooms, Department of State, Washington D.C., Gift of Mr and Mrs Mitchell Toradash: 71 above (Helga Studio photo)
Germanisches National Museum: 51 below
Giraudon: 35 above left, 57 right, 82-83
Greenfield Village and Henry Ford Museum: 49 above and below (Helga Studio photo)
Helga Studio, New York: 65 (Private Collection)
Hirmer Fotoarchiv, Munich: 10 (Galerie d'Apollon, Louvre), 37, 40 below left (by gracious permission of H.M. the Queen), 58, 74 (by gracious permission of H.M. the Queen)
Michael Holford: 12 (Villa Giulia, Rome), 14-15, 16 above left and right, 17, 21 below right, 38 above, 38-39
Angelo Hornak: 11, 19 above, 30, 36 right, 54 below, 80, 88 right and below, 91 above and below

London Museum: 77 left
Metropolitan Museum of Art: 81 (Purchase, Mrs Paul Moore Gift 1965), 86 (Gift of Mrs R. Sage, Bequest of Ethel Yocum, Bequest of Charlotte E. Hoadley, Rogers Fund, by exchange), 87 below (The Edgar J. Kaufmann Charitable Foundation Fund, 1968)
Minneapolis Institute of Arts: 75 above
National Museum, Nuremberg: 51 below
National Trust, Clandon Park (photos M. Dyer Associates): 2-3, 32, 35 below, 45, 47 above and below, 48 above, 50 above and below, 51 above, 52-53, 68 below left and right, 69, 71 below, 72-73 all, 75 left and below right, 83 below
Phoebus Picture Library: 35 above right, 36 left, 38 above, 42-43, 60 right, 77 left, 85 above and below, 88 above left
Private Collection (photo M. Dyer Associates): 33 below left, 59 centre, 67 above and below, 94 left
Scala: 6-7, 9, 19 below, 20, 22, 23 right, 25, 28-29, 33 above and below right, 34, 40 above, 51 below, 53 above and below, 60 left, 78-79
Victoria & Albert Museum: 11, 16 above left, 19 above, 23 below, 24 above and below, 30, 31, 36 left and right, 38-39, 54 below, 88 below, 91 above, 92 below right
Werner Forman: 8, 15 below
Jeremy Whitaker: 62-63, 68 above, 83 above